Library of
Davidson College

THE SECRET SYSTEM

THE SECRET SYSTEM

A STUDY IN THE CHRONOLOGY OF THE OLD TESTAMENT

BY

GERHARD LARSSON

LEIDEN
E. J. BRILL
1973

ISBN 90 04 03667 9

Copyright 1973 by E. J. Brill, Leiden, Netherlands

All rights reserved. No part of this book may be reproduced or translated in any form, by print, photoprint, microfilm, microfiche or any other means without written permission from the publisher

PRINTED IN THE NETHERLANDS

CONTENTS

Preface VII

- I. The Mysterious Chronology 1
- II. Finding a System 7
- III. The System against the Chronological Background . . 12
- IV. Mathematical and Statistical Tests 19
- V. The Question of Right Seasons 25
- VI. The Concealed Meanings of Dates 31
- VII. Periods in the System 39
- VIII. The System and the History 44
- IX. When Was the Chronology Created? 51
- X. Modifications in the Chronology 56
- XI. Ideological Content and Connections with Other Sources 65
- XII. A Hypothesis about the Canon 74

Appendix 91

PREFACE

This is a book dealing with a rather special subject. Can the chronology of the Old Testament really be very interesting? Of course, there are always people who specialize in these things, but their number is pretty small. And after all there have been so many books and articles about these problems, without the discussion leading to any conclusive solution, only to more hypotheses. The actual situation in this field is in fact a little embarrassing.

Is it really so important if we succeed in solving some problems about which year one king in Israel died or another king in Judah ascended the throne? Certainly this may be of value to a student of ancient history, but its general importance seems limited. The possibility of making definite datings with the aid of the Old Testament may also be questioned.

Personally—not being a specialist in these things—I would not have given them much thought, not have found them particularly interesting and especially not have devoted considerable time to scrutinizing another person's theories about them, had it not been for one thing. The originator of these theories, Mr Knut Stenring, does not claim that they are just one possible solution. He is very definite that they give *the* solution, not of the real chronology but of the *system* used in the main parts of the Old Testament. Another of his claims is that this solution is of much more importance than just to provide a better dating. We shall see some of the circumstances in connection with the creation of the first Bible canon and learn the almost exact date of this event. The solution explains many dark points in the texts, is of obvious value for textual criticism and gives a better idea of some of the underlying ideas. In addition, there is the fascinating conclusion that the chronology forms a secret system, deliberately hidden by the men who designed it.

As secrets are a challenge, attracting us to find out the truth behind them, this was perhaps the source of my interest. Even my first tests—made as a part of the examination needed when financial support from scientific funds for the printing of Stenring's investigation was applied for—turned out to strongly support the hypothesis. Further tests were made and I may as well confess that these tests quite convinced me. The proofs of Stenring's results are to me quite conclusive. I may as well admit this straight away, as there is no point in playing games with my readers and saving this information to the last page.

The reason why I have reached this conviction does not depend on any persuasion on Stenring's part. His book *The Enclosed Garden* just presents the bare facts. The reader himself has to find the proofs. The main reason for publishing the present book is that, as I have devoted much work to testing the hypotheses, I may as well present the results and save the labour of others interested in this subject. As my own background is essentially a mathematical one but most of my viewpoints touch on other subjects, I should be grateful if the specialists in these subjects would give them careful consideration. Here I would like to express my gratitude to Dr A. Carlson at the Department of Old Testament Study, University of Upsala, who has kindly read and commented my manuscript.

My intention is, however, not to write only for the scholar. In my opinion the results are of general interest, as they give a partly new view of the amalgamation of the nucleus of the Old Testament. Therefore in this book I sometimes mention and even try to explain things which are well known to the specialists. I beg their indulgence for this.

The important thing to me is that not all my readers should find the ideas peculiar, though possible, and stop at that. I have seen too many reviews of exegetical works end with a vague declaration. Because of this, I should like as many of my readers as possible to try and make up their minds—positively or negatively—so we might gradually come to a conclusion as to what is likely and what is not. We are badly in need of more generally accepted standpoints concerning chronology, from which further steps will be possible.

Stockholm, January 1973   GERHARD LARSSON

Professor at the Royal Institute
of Technology

CHAPTER ONE

THE MYSTERIOUS CHRONOLOGY

In the old days each book in the Bible was looked upon as a unit, mostly written at one time and by a single writer. Many people still believe this. However, the scientific view has changed. Most of the books are now considered as products of often a long development. One of the main objects of the exegesis of the Old Testament (OT) is to clarify this development and shed light on the original sources to which the different texts belong.

Sources of the OT

This analysis uses different tools. One is to scrutinize the style—the vocabulary, the modes of expression, the linguistic features, etc. Marked differences are often easily visible and may be an indication that the book in question was compiled from different sources. There may likewise be differences in the religious and political views. Often there are duplications. The same course of events, for example, the Creation, is related twice in different ways and thereby indicates a heterogeneous origin.

Considerations like these have led to the nowadays commonly accepted theory that the central parts of the OT are the results of redactions, in which separate written sources or streams of tradition are amalgamated into units. The first four books in the Bible—Genesis, Exodus, Leviticus and Numbers—are mostly thought to have been composed from at any rate three original works of traditions: the Yahwist (*J*), the Elohist (*E*) and the Priestly (*P*) sources.[1]

The *J* source is supposed to be the oldest and is distinguished by its clear and direct style, the keen characterization of the persons involved and of the earth-centred world, where man and Yahweh are both reduced to human scale, acting together in an intense drama. *E*

---

[1] Cf., for example, O. Eissfeldt, *Einleitung in das Alte Test.*, M. Noth, *Überlieferungsgeschichte des Pentateuch*, I. Engnell, *Gamla Testamentet*, E. Nielsen, *Oral Tradition*, E. A. Speiser, *Genesis* (The Anchor Bible), J. G. Vink, The Date and Origin of the Priestly Code in the Old Testament, *Oudtest. Studiën* XV (1969), 1-144, etc.

is in many ways related to and sometimes difficult to distinguish from *J*. In *E* the direct interaction between man and God is often replaced by the interposition of angels, dreams, etc. In *J* the actions speak for themselves, in *E* there is a tendency to explain them. *E* sometimes tells parallel but often distinctly different narratives from *J*.

The author of *P* has a very strong interest in genealogical details and relates in ages and years the unbroken chain of the generations through which God's promises were handed down. The world in *P* is heaven-centered, and the author has little interest in individuals. What really matters is the formal relations between God and the human being—a priestly view. This source, as a whole, is mostly thought to be considerably later than the others (later than the Exile).

The fifth book in our Bible—Deuteronomy—is supposed to have been written by a group of reformist priests, the Deuteronomists or the *D* group, perhaps shortly before the time of the Babylonian Captivity or perhaps later. Characteristic of the group is its demand for the centralization of the cult in one place, Jerusalem, and its interpretation of Israel's history as an alternation between periods of blessing, when Israel obeyed the will of God, and periods of disobedience and cursing. The redaction of the books from Joshua to II Kings is also often attributed to the *D* group.[2]

There are further redactions to be considered. For example, some exegetes look upon Chronicles, Ezra and Nehemiah as having been mainly written by a single writer or group of writers. This writer or writers were especially interested in the priestly and ritualistic aspects and stress the role of Jerusalem and the central cult there. However, there are different opinions as to whether this portion of the OT really is a homogeneous work and not the result of a compilation from several sources.[3]

Even more Bible redactions have been claimed. However, many exegetes have a feeling that this is going too far, that the Bible is too much broken into pieces in this way. They prefer to talk of different traditions or oral elements, which have gradually been written down and brought together, perhaps in one or two final redactions. But also these scholars are quite aware that there are distinct groups or streams of tradition behind the OT text.[4]

---

[2] R. A. Carlson, *David the Chosen King* (intro.) and others.

[3] Cf., on the one hand, C. Torrey, *The Chronicler's History of Israel*, and, on the other, S. Mowinckel, *Studien zu dem Buche Ezra-Nehemia*.

[4] S. Engnell, op. cit.

The details of this problem will not be discussed here. The important thing is that we do not have in the OT a collection of separate books written by individual writers, but several sources, both oral and written, which have been amalgamated in a more or less complicated redactional process, very likely in different stages.

Stenring's hypothesis

Against this background Stenring's[5] hypothesis does not seem sensational or incredible *per se*. The hypothesis is that there was one concluding redaction embracing twelve books: Genesis, Exodus, Leviticus, Numbers, Deuteronomy, Joshua, Judges, I-II Samuel, I-II Kings, I-II Chronicles (including Ezra 1.1-3.7), Jeremiah and Ezekiel. These twelve books constituted the first Bible canon. One of the connecting elements was the chronology.

As I have just said, this is not too sensational a hypothesis. But if it is true, it is interesting and will give us a picture of the way in which the central part of the Old Testament was formed.

The sensational fact, however, is that this chronology seems to have been deliberately hidden. There are very definite signs that it was not meant as something for the common man but as a secret for the initiated. Another very interesting thing is that the date of the final redaction seems to be fairly definitely fixed (around 230-235 B.C.). Interesting, too, is the high degree of elaboration of the chronology, a feature connected with its secret character. Before discussing the system in detail, I shall very briefly mention some of the problems which have confronted scholars concerned with this subject.

Earlier works on the OT chronology

It is certainly not due to any lack of effort that the problems of biblical chronology are not yet solved. They have in fact been given much thought for two thousand years. Pre-Christian and early Christian writers tried to fit all the given dates into a perfect system. Sometimes they thought they had found the solution. Less than 100 years after the beginning of the Christian era, Josephus gave exact figures for the important events of the OT.[6] In the Talmud[7] all the

---

[5] A very short, preliminary edition of Stenring's work, containing tables and some diagrams, was issued in 1952. The full edition is K. Stenring, *The Enclosed Garden*, Almqvist & Wiksell, Stockholm 1966. Some essential points are summarized in G. Larsson: Is Biblical Chronology Systematic or not, Rev. de Qumran, no. 24.

[6] Josephus, *Jewish Antiquities*.   [7] *Seder 'Olam Rabbah*.

years from the Creation to the Exodus and from the building of the Temple to the destruction of Jerusalem are given. The Jewish era (still in use) is thus founded on the supposed time from the Creation.

Africanus, Eusebius and other Christian chronologists worked out detailed systems from the Bible and tried to fit them into the chronology of the heathen world. Their efforts seemed in many ways to be successful and their results were widely accepted, though not altogether. The struggle with the biblical years and dates went on all through the centuries. The best known of the later systems is that of the Irish archbishop, James Ussher, published around 1650,[8] which starts with the Creation and continues to the fall of Jerusalem and the Babylonian Captivity. The results seemed so trustworthy that Ussher's dating was placed in the margin of the famous English Bible of 1701.

Even though many looked upon this system as the true biblical chronology, it could not solve all the problems. In fact, they gradually seemed to increase. A great many scholars up to the present day have tried different solutions.[9] and interest in these things seems to have grown more and more, perhaps because the discoveries of the Dead Sea Scrolls have revealed how important calendars and time reckoning were for the Jews at the period around the birth of Christ. But still we have no generally accepted system. In fact, the solutions often differ substantially.

Some problems

How can this be, when we have so many exact figures given in the OT? It is remarkable how much attention is devoted to chronological information in the OT, seemingly far more than in other historical writings and narratives from the same period. Not only years but also dates are given, even for events in the very remotest times. Especially in Genesis, the author apparently makes an effort to link up the generations in a continuous genealogical chain, by systematically

---

[8] J. Ussher, *Annales Veteris et Novi Testamenti*.

[9] Especially the time of the divided kingdom has been treated in many studies, such as J. Wellhausen, *Die Zeitrechnung des Buches der Könige seit der Teilung des Reiches* (1875), A. Kamphausen, *Die Chronologie der hebräischen Könige* (1883), F. X. Kugler, *Von Moses bis Paulus* (1922), J. Lewy, *Die Chronologie der Könige von Israel und Juda* (1927), J. Begrich, *Die Chronologie der Könige von Israel und Juda* (1929), E. Thiele, *The Mysterious Numbers of the Hebrew Kings* (1951), A. Jepsen, Zur Chronologie der Könige von Israel und Juda (*ZAW* 1964), and W. Wifall, The Chronology of the Divided Monarchy of Israel (*ZAW* 1968).

giving the age of the father at the birth of his first son. And in the Books of Kings and Chronicles there is a complete list of the kings of Israel and Judah, together with the lengths of their reigns. Furthermore, synchronisms are given for the accessions of the kings of Israel and Judah, in terms of the corresponding dates of the accessions of the rulers of the other nation. Besides, long intervals are stated, such as that the sojourn of the children of Israel in Egypt lasted 430 years, that Solomon started to build the Temple in the 480th year after Exodus, etc. With such a lot of information, it should not be too difficult to establish an approximate system, perhaps not historically true but in agreement with the Bible itself.

The trouble is, however, that so much of the biblical information seems self-contradictory. In one place we are told that Ahaziah of Judah came to the throne in the twelfth year of Joram of Israel (II Kings 8.25) but one chapter later we are told that it was in the eleventh year (II Kings 9.29). The synchronisms very often do not fit in with the given reigns of the kings. To cite Professor Thiele,[10] who is an expert on these things:

> Perhaps the greatest single difficulty of Old Testament chronology is found in the seeming disagreement between the synchronisms and the lengths of reign. Every scholar who was endeavored to work out a chronological pattern based upon both the synchronisms and the lengths of reign knows something of the extreme difficulties involved. If a chronology is worked out according to the lengths of reign, then the synchronisms will not fit; and if the synchronisms are employed, then it appears that the lengths of reign must be discarded. The two sets of data just do not seem to fit one into the other.

Many other examples of contradictions can be given. For instance, Noah begot Shem at the age of 500 years and entered the Ark the year in which he became 600. But Shem was still 100 years old when he begot Arphachshad 2 years *after* the Deluge (Gen. 11.10). In one place (II Kings 25.8) we are told that Nebuzaradan arrived in Jerusalem and burnt the city on the seventh day of the fifth month, in another (Jer. 52.12) that it was on the tenth day. Otherwise the events are described in almost identical terms and therefore the difference in this very important date is striking. Exactly the same can be said about the event described in II Kings 25.27 and Jer. 52.31. In Jer. 52.11 it is said that Jerusalem was destroyed in Nebuchadnezzar's 19th year but later

---

[10] Thiele, op. cit., p. 7.

in the same chapter that the prisoners from Jerusalem were carried away in his 18th year. And so on.

Why these contradictions? It is, of course, always possible to say that the books of the Bible were compiled from different sources or that misinterpretations and scribal errors may have occurred. But in that case would these very obvious contradictions have been left unrectified? The discoveries of the Dead Sea Scrolls have also shown with what meticulous care the books were handed down through the centuries.

As I have said, the OT gives the greatest attention to chronological information, which was obviously regarded as very important. Against this background the mixture of precise information and the apparently random and negligent treatment of this information is difficult to explain. The contradictions sometimes seem almost too obvious and provocative, as if the writer of the text were hinting that this cannot be true from a common sense point of view. But, as the Scripture cannot be wrong, there must be a hidden secret.

It is interesting in this connection to note that the tradition of hidden secrets in the Scriptures has existed in Jewish mysticism for perhaps two thousand years under the name of the *Cabbala*. In the Cabbala great stress was laid on chronological information, the numerical significance of names, sacred numbers, etc. The existence of so active a tradition of a hidden meaning in the Scriptures cannot be neglected.

Let us suppose that all these figures of years and dates really were important for the final redactors and were constructed with much care, as far as possible on the basis of the historical sources known to them. Let us suppose further that the contradictions are not mistakes but have a meaning and that we must reckon with the possibility that at any rate part of this meaning was deliberately hidden. To what hypotheses and conclusions would such a view lead? This was Stenring's approach.

CHAPTER TWO

FINDING A SYSTEM

In attempting to find a system, it is quite natural to start by assuming that the information given is correct and to consider what this assumption will lead to. If the result is not likely, the hypothesis is rejected. So Stenring assumed that the chronological dates given in the Hebrew (Massoretic) version of the OT were correct, not always historically, of course, but as part of a system. It was a daring hypothesis when it was made some 40 years ago. Nowadays, after the finding of the scrolls of the Qumran community in the Dead Sea desert, it seems much more likely. Professor Thiele and other scholars have started from the same hypothesis that the dates are the same as once given.

Calendars used

In that case there does not seem to be any other way to explain the obvious contradictions about dates than to assume that two or more calendars were used. How can it otherwise be true, for example, that Nebuzaradan arrived in Jerusalem and destroyed it on both the seventh and the tenth days of the fifth month?

The assumption is, in fact, not at all impossible. It is a historical fact that many calendars were in use in those days and that even double datings in letters etc. were not uncommon. Several scholars have also reckoned with the possibility that more than one calendar was used in the Bible.

But which calendars? And how many of them? This could not be known in advance. Of course, it was not likely that any of these calendars was a lunar-solar calendar, which used lunar months but now and then intercalated an extra month to keep the right season. In those days such calendars were dependent on actual observations, were normally somewhat irregular and could not easily be used in a system stretching over thousands of years. They must therefore have been schematic but regular lunar or solar calendars. The best test of a hypothesis is that it fits. So Stenring tried different calendars in actual use at that time.

There is no need to discuss here the heavy work that was involved in such trials. It is sufficient to say that gradually three calendars seemed to give a possible explanation. All these calendars were in use in the centuries before Christ. At this point Stenring's hypothesis could be stated as follows.

The chronological data given in the sections of the Bible concerned are taken from three calendars, whose origins were fixed at the beginning of the first day of Creation and which thereafter ran parallel. Of these calendars, one is based on the ancient lunar year of 354 days, one on the Egyptian solar year of 365 days and one on the "standard" year (a solar year where 4 years = 4 × 365 + 1 day). They were employed in the normal way, the lunar year consisting of 12 months of 29 and 30 days alternately,[11] the Egyptian solar year consisting of 12 months of 30 days followed by 5 intercalary days, and the standard year with one extra intercalated day every fourth year (the form we meet with in the Canopus Decree).[12] In the luni-solar calendar, special months were intercalated with the aid of direct observations, in order to compensate the differences between the lunar and the solar years; however, this compensating process was *not* employed in the chronological system of the original OT, which was quite natural, as corrections did not follow a regular pattern at this time.

An item of chronological information in the OT may be derived from any of these calendars. A certain variation was, of course, one of the chief means of keeping the system from the knowledge of the uninitiated. However, it later turned out that the information as to years followed a specific pattern. It normally referred to lunar years until the period of the kings (though with important exceptions in connection with the Exodus and the Wandering in the Wilderness), and to solar years in the following period until the division of the kingdom, after which standard years were used until the return from

---

[11] In the ancient Jewish calendar, used in the centuries before the birth of Christ, the beginning of a new month was fixed by observation of the new moon. Thus, there were in practice irregularities, so that months of 29 and 30 days did not always change regularly. Enoch 78 : 15-16 (probably from the 2nd century B.C.) indicates clearly that at this time both a lunar year of 354 days and a solar year of 365 days existed among the Jews.

[12] The calendar in question, the Tanitic calendar, was introduced into Egypt by the decision in 238 B.C. of a great assembly of priests. It is not quite clear how long this calendar was in use. It was very similar to the Julian calendar, using the same principle for deciding the length of the solar year.

Captivity, when the chronological system came to an end. Ezekiel, however, uses the lunar year as a rule.

OTHER FEATURES OF THE SYSTEM

Most of the chronological information in the Bible is not given in months and days but in years. How can years be combined so that they give exact calendar dates of the type used in the Bible? The answer is obvious: only if they are handled as *exact* years it is possible to start from a date, to add a few years and to arrive at another date. So Stenring assumed that the chronological information is to be read exactly as it stands in the text. Thus, if a period of 5 years is mentioned, this means 5 years to the day. Naturally this is normally not in agreement with the historical facts, but in a system of mathematical design which claims to be exact, it is essential that every period mentioned should have a fixed length.

There has been much discussion about the point from which a king started to count the years of his reign—whether it was from the time of his actual accession, from the New Year before his accession or from the New Year after it. Different systems were used in different countries and we still do not know which methods were preferred in Israel and Judah. Very likely the redactors of the Bible did not know either; they were probably working several hundred years later than the reigns of these kings.[13] And even though the system was known, it could not be used for constructing a chronology, in so far as the exact dates of the kings' accessions were not known. So the simplest thing was to assume that no post- or ante-dating was used in the last

---

[13] Thus, for example, Thiele supposes that in Israel the non-accession-year system (reckoning the regnal years from the New Year before the accession) was used from the division of the kingdom to Jehoash and then changed to the accession-year system (reckoning from the New Year after). Judah, on the contrary, is supposed to have used the accession-year system from the beginning, then to have changed to non-accession during the reign of Jehoram and then to have changed again during the reign of Amaziah. Wifall (*ZAW* 1968 : 3) reckons that there were later alterations by the redactor of the chronology: "The original chronology of the divided monarchy was post-dated for both periods. This first post-dated chronology was altered, so that period one (before Jehu) began one year later for the kings of Israel than for the kings of Judah, and so that the chronological data for the reigns of Athaliah and Ahaz of Judah was omitted from the chronology of period two. Subsequently an editor attempted to restore the original text of Kings and to correct and restore the chronology through the use of ante-dating". Thus, Wifall, like Stenring, makes a sharp difference between what really happened and how the chronology was explained and adapted several hundred years later. According to him, the difference between the events and the system explains much of the confusion in the chronology.

reconstruction of the chronology but that the regnal years were just added together. Those regnal years were probably taken from the old chronicles.

But it cannot be as simple as that. The dates do not fit. If we add all the reigns of the kings of Judah up to a certain event and then do the same with the kings of Israel, the numbers of years mostly differ.[14] If we still accept that the dates of the reigns are not corrupted, then we must assume that there were co-regents or possibly interregnums. Most scholars have done so. Sometimes the OT actually mentions co-regency. Solomon, for example, was made king some time before David died. In such cases we do not know from which year the reign of a king is given. It may be the year when he became co-regent, but it may also be the year when he became sole king.

We may also note that the exact interpretation of periods of time gives a double meaning to expressions like "in the fifth year of his reign". This expression may refer both to 4 full years after the accession to the throne and to 5 full years and also, of course, to the period between them. In the chronology, however, it appears, that the first two were the alternatives mainly employed. This fact explains a number of the "contradictions".

As an example, I may quote the much-discussed passage in Gen. 2.2: "An on the *seventh* day God ended his work". The last of the works of creation—the creation of man—took place on the *sixth* day. Owing to this apparent contradiction, the creation of Adam—and with it the births and deaths of all the patriarchs—has formally been assigned to the hour of sunset (the period "between the two evenings", as the Septuagint expresses it), which was simultaneously part of the sixth and part of the seventh day. The Samaritan and the Septuagint versions of the Bible use "the sixth day", which here appears to be a later emendation designed to bridge over something difficult to explain.[15]

To summarize, the following were the main features of the system which Stenring found:

[14] Cf. Thiele, op. cit., p. 6.

[15] As an example of the different explanations on this point, I quote the Anchor Bible: "Since the task of creation was finished on the sixth day, the text can hardly go on to say that God concluded it on the seventh day. It follows therefore that (*a*) the numeral is an error for "sixth", as assumed by LXX, Sam., and other versions; (*b*) the pertinent verb is to be interpreted as a pluperfect: God had finished on the sixth day and rested on the seventh; or (*c*) the verb carries some more particular shade of meaning".

(1) Three calendars, starting from the first day of Creation.

(2) The exact meaning of each piece of chronological information given in the above-mentioned parts of the OT in its Hebrew (Massoretic) version.

(3) The possibilities of the co-regency of kings.

(4) The possibilities that the reign of a king may be calculated alternatively from the date when his co-regency started or from the date when he became sole king.

The rest was application, even though the solution was often hard to find. There was especially a need for the most critical scrutiny of every chronological indication given, carefully considering the different possible alternatives. This was of the utmost importance, as everything indicates that the system was deliberately hidden and that the redactors sometimes tried to throw the readers off the scent.

The solution found can be studied in Appendix 2. But, of course, nobody can accept the bare statement that this is the solution. It must be tested and proved. In the following chapters I shall try to give the main observations, which have convinced me. I start with a general discussion as to whether the system is trustworthy against the general chronological background and then go on to more exact tests.

CHAPTER THREE

THE SYSTEM AGAINST THE CHRONOLOGICAL BACKGROUND

In dealing with ancient history, we are only too apt to judge the events and thoughts of that time against the background of our own. Of course, we are theoretically aware that this is a fault but in practice we fail time after time to take it into account. So some of the points in the proposed chronological system may seem to us a little confusing and to have no connection with religion. Perhaps we get a feeling that this playing with figures and dates is mere jugglery, unworthy of the redactors of the holy Scriptures. But we may understand these things better, if we try to see them as people did in ancient times.

THE IMPORTANCE OF CALENDARS AND DATES

Firstly, the enormous importance assigned to time reckoning and calendars must be emphasized. In the Babylonian culture there was a strong feeling for the magic of numbers, calendars and chronology. Each god had his special number, the names of gods were given to the days of the week and the months of the year, and the calendars were connected with the heavenly bodies and thus with the gods. Similar ideas appeared in Egypt. The calendar was an extremely important thing and was entrusted to the priests. When a new Pharaoh ascended the throne, he had to swear a solemn oath not to alter or confuse the time reckoning.[16] In the hellenistic world astrology soon became a serious manifestation of the belief in a magical interplay between the heavenly bodies, the chronological data and the destinies of men.

It is quite obvious that also among the Jews time reckoning and calendars were of great religious importance. It was the duty of the Sanhedrin to fix the beginning of a new year and a new month.[17] The priests also had the responsibility of making sure that the feasts fell on the right days. We may learn from the OT itself what stress was laid on the exact day of the Passover, the Feast of Unleavened Bread,

---

[16] R. Parker, *The Calendars of Ancient Egypt*.
[17] J. Finegan, *Handbook of Biblical Chronology*, p. 40.

the Feast of Tabernacles, and so on. It is remarkable how often exact dates are given in the text.

This general importance of calendars and time is very strongly emphasized in the pseudepigraphic Jewish literature dating from the centuries around the birth of Christ, such as the Book of Enoch and the Book of Jubilees. The former lays stress on Enoch as the keeper of the secrets of the heavenly bodies and the right calendar, and warns of a time when chronological reckoning will be distorted by evil men. In the Book of Jubilees, the whole sacred history is built up on periods of years (jubilees) of 49 years and chronology is thus given the role of the main connecting element. Besides, all important events fall again and again on the same main feast-days. The continued tradition has been illustrated by the findings at Qumran. Questions concerning the calendar seem to have been of major significance to the Qumran sect—perhaps this was one of the main points in its opposition to official Judaism—and numbers as a whole seem to have been regarded as expressing the divine order.[18] In later works from the first centuries A.D. chronology often seems to conceal a secret meaning, for example, of an eschatological nature.[19] This tradition is continued in the Talmud and the Cabbala, where chronological information, the numerical meanings of names, sacred numbers, etc. have a deep significance.[20]

There is no need to go further in the exemplification, as the evidence of the importance and holy character of calendars, dates and chronology also in the Jewish world is overwhelming. So we may safely conclude that, if a redactor of the Scriptures was seeking a strong connecting element between the different parts, it would have been hard to find a more meaningful and more awe-inspiring element than chronology. And why not make it still more meaningful by concealing it from the eyes of the uninitiated? Was it not in fact dangerous for impure men to be exposed to all the holiness and secrecy of the Scriptures?

Use of parallel calendars and exact years

Even so, is it not rather odd to use different calendars and to alternate between them without mentioning the alternations? Let us

---

[18] J. Finegan, op. cit., p. 44.
[19] J. Meysing, L'énigme de la chronologie biblique et qumrânienne dans une nouvelle lumière, *Rev. de Qumr.*, 1967.
[20] Cf., for example, the Jewish Encyclopaedia under the word *gematria*.

first stress the well-known fact that it was very common to use more than one calendar in the same country. The Babylonians did so and so did other peoples. We know that in Egypt several calendars were used in parallel and that double datings in letters, edicts, etc. were common, sometimes without any indication from which calendar a date was taken.[21] Both lunar and solar calendars were in use at the same time, as well as foreign calendars. In the centuries B.C. we thus often find datings with one date in the Macedonian and another date in the Egyptian (civil) solar calendar.

From the pseudepigraphic writings and from the Qumran scrolls it is clear that different calendars were also in use in Palestine. We have, for example, one calendar in the Books of Enoch and Jubilees and in the Qumran scrolls and another that was accepted by official Judaism. Also foreign calendars — such as the Babylonian and the Egyptian — were well known. Many scholars believe that in ancient Israel there were one or more changes between the solar and lunar calendars.[22] In that case they very probably ran in parallel for some time. Hanhart has demonstrated that probably two calendars were used in the Books of the Maccabees.[23] Changes between them are made without the slightest indication in the text. On the whole, it was common in the ancient world to reckon both by a civil calendar and by a calendar of religious festivals. The Qumran sect, for example, seems to have had the Babylonian calendar for daily use but a calendar of its own in religious connections. In the same way, the Jews of Egypt used both a civil Egyptian solar year and a religious lunar year in their calendars. Against this background, therefore, it is not particularly surprising that the chronological system should be based on three calendars.

What about the method of letting one year in the text mean one year exactly and one day mean one day to the hour? Is not that too theoretical a construction? Of course, it can very seldom have been historically true that a king started his reign on a given date and ended it on the same date some years later. But such constructions have to

---

[21] A. E. Samuel, *Ptolemaic Chronology* (1962).

[22] J. Morgenstern has thus argued in several papers that Israel during the period of the divided kingdom mainly had calendars based on the solar year. Finegan (op. cit.) is of the same opinion. J. B. Segal (Intercalation and the Hebrew calendar, *Vet. Test.* 1957) opposes this and argues that the lunar calendar even then was the basis of the time reckoning.

[23] R. Hanhart, Zur Zeitrechnung des I und II Makkabäerbuches, *Beiheft 88 zur Zeitsch. f. Altt. Wiss.*

be made in a formally exact system. It is also easy to show that this method of interpreting round periods of time as exact measures was applied by classical historians. When, for example, the Jewish historian Josephus adds together a number of reigns consisting mainly of whole numbers of years but mixed with months, the chronological data are treated as exact numbers and the total is given in years and months.[24] No regard is paid to whether there was any pre- or post-dating concerning the lengths of the reigns. We find the same method in the works of other ancient writers.[25] On the whole, we may say that this is quite a natural method if we want a formally fixed chronology but do not know the exact dates of accession.[26]

Co-regencies

As I mentioned earlier, two other main features in the system are the possibilities of the co-regency of kings and that the reign of a king can be calculated either from the date when his co-regency started or from the date when he became sole king. It is easy to find parallels to these things. In those days co-regency was common in the whole of the Orient. Many examples are known from Babylonian, Assyrian and Tyrenic chronicles.[27] In some Egyptian dynasties co-regency was the normal thing. It was also common in Ptolemaic Egypt.[28] The Bible itself tells us explicitly that David made Solomon king in David's own lifetime. Some other co-regencies are also hinted at.

Furthermore, we can find examples of different ways of giving the years of a king's reign. In some Egyptian chronicles the years given include the years of co-regency but in others not. Sometimes the method changes within the same chronicle—without any mention of the fact.[29] The same confusion is found in edicts and letters of this period. In contemporary papyri dating from the time of Ptolemy II,

---

[24] For example, see Josephus, *Contra Apionem*, I : 121-126.

[25] Such as Manetho, Africanus, and Eusebius.

[26] In my opinion C. R. Driver's criticism of Stenring on this point (*Journ. of Theol. Studies* 1967, p. 187) is therefore wrong.

[27] Perhaps a more common practice than co-regencies in Babylon and Assyria was to officially instal the successor as crown prince. The difference between this and real co-regency was probably not great. The OT speaks of Nebuchadnezzar as already king at the battle of Charchemish (Jer. 46.2), when he was still crown prince.

[28] Thus, Ptolemy I and Ptolemy II were co-regents for some years.

[29] In the Ptolemaic Canon co-regency is reckoned to the successor, which also seems to be the case in Manetho's chronicle concerning the later dynasties but not the earlier ones. In the Turin Papyrus (around 1200 B.C.) the period of the co-regency seems mostly to be included in the reign of the first Pharaoh.

the scribes give the date sometimes reckoned from the beginning of the king's co-regency and sometimes reckoned from the beginning of his sole regency, but they do not tell us from which point they are calculating.[30]

THE MYSTIQUE OF NUMBERS AND DATES

Another thing that may seem a little odd to us is the play with figures and the magic of certain numbers, as well as the symbolism of certain dates. But this is nothing new in the chronology of the Bible. The whole ancient world was soaked in these ideas. In the Greek-Hellenistic sphere we may refer to Pythagoras and his doctrine of numbers, in which numbers were the true reality, and to the mystique and the secret societies which grew up in the wake of the Pythagoreans. This influence was also strong in the Jewish world in the centuries just before the birth of Christ. Thus, it is obvious how great a similarity there was between many late Jewish ideas and customs and those of the Pythagoreans.[31] Much of the thinking in the pseudepigraphic literature can also be traced to the same source. The importance of numbers and their symbolism is clearly demonstrated in the use of *gematria*, in which there is a connection between numbers and letters and in which words with the same numerical value are more or less identified in a mystical way.[32] We can find examples of this in the Bible and still more in later Jewish literature.

But is it not incredible that some redactors of the Scriptures should try to conceal the system and for some reason even let many things appear as contradictions? Sacred and secret had much in common in the ancient world. It was almost a self-evident proposition that the most sacred things should be a mystery to the temple. The Pythagorean brotherhoods kept silent about their secrets, which were often connected with the deeper meanings of numbers. Nobody but the High Priest himself was allowed to go into the Holy of Holies in the Temple of Jerusalem. And when, according to what is related in IV Esdras, Esdras had written all the holy books at the dictation of the Highest, he was told (14.45-48):

> 45. And it came to pass, when the forty days were fulfilled, that the Highest spoke, saying, The first that thou hast written publish openly, that the worthy and unworthy may read it:

---

[30] Samuel, op. cit.
[31] I. Lévy, *La légende de Pythagore de Grèce en Palestine* (1926).
[32] See the Jewish Encyclopaedia.

46. But keep the seventy last, that thou mayest deliver them only to such as be wise among the people:

47. For in them is the spring of understanding, the fountain of wisdom, and the stream of knowledge.

48. And I did so.

It is obvious that chronology, as such, was a thing that normally was reserved for the wise and was not meant to be understood by the unworthy. It was always handled by the priests. In Babylon, in Persia, in Egypt and in Israel the priests determined the calendars and kept a reckoning of the time. How secret this was can still be seen in the Dead Sea Scrolls, where secret writing was used in manuscripts with astrological and chronological contents. That secret writing, as such, is not unknown in the Bible itself can be seen in several examples (cf. Jer. 51.1). And in the late Jewish writings there is a strong tradition that special secrets—often connected with dates and numbers—were hidden in the Scriptures.

Other chronological systems

One thing which may seem peculiar is that the Jews in particular should try to create such a system in these early days of historical science. We know that chronicles were written in Israel as well as in other countries. But it is a long step from separate chronicles to intricate systems. Let us then remember that 200-300 B.C. was a period when chronological systems were developed for all the leading peoples in the Orient. The Babylonian priest Berossus wrote around 260-270 B.C. his famous Babylonian-Chaldean chronicle, which, like Genesis, starts with ten long-lived and legendary kings or patriarchs before the Deluge and is carried down to almost his own time. The Egyptian priest Manetho, who was almost a contemporary of Berossus compiled a list of Egyptian kings, starting with gods and demi-gods. In both systems there are striking parallels with the chronology of the OT. Around 240 B.C. Eratosthenes, the Hellenistic scientist and the principal librarian of the great library of Alexandria, compiled a chronology from the fall of Troy down to his own time, a chronology which was to be the foundation of almost all later chronological writings about that period. With the close connection in the third century B.C. between Palestine and both Babylonia and Egypt—especially Alexandria—it is quite understandable that the idea of chronological systems should influence the redactors of the Hebrew Scriptures.

Such ideas would also serve a national purpose very well. Chronologists such as Berossus and Manetho worked at a time when their peoples were oppressed and humiliated by foreign conquerors and obviously tried to emphasize the great history and the antiquity of their peoples with the object of strengthening their wills. Josephus had the same purpose, when, a few hundred years later, he wrote his Jewish history.[33] Indeed, such a purpose would be a strong motive for including a chronological system in the OT, which in so many other respects is written with the purpose of rallying and educating the Jewish people by pointing out their history.

As a conclusion we may say that none of the principles used in the chronological system in the form presented by Stenring seems unlikely against the background of the time. On the contrary, it is easy to find the same or similar methods in actual use in writings dating from that period. Furthermore we find that, at the same time as the system was probably constructed, other systems were being constructed in the same cultural sphere, often by priests and with a religious and national purpose. We also know that calendars and chronology were fundamental elements in much of the pseudepigraphic, Talmudic and Cabbalistic writings in the later Jewish tradition and also that in this tradition the idea of hidden secrets in the Scriptures was very prevalent.

[33] Josephus, *Contra Apionem*, I : 1.

CHAPTER FOUR

MATHEMATICAL AND STATISTICAL TESTS

The discussion so far has been of a general nature, with the main objective of finding if there is anything incredible in the hypothesis as such or in the special methods used. I shall now take the investigation a step further and concentrate on the positive proofs of Stenring's results. I shall first try purely mathematical and statistical tests.

Does the solution fit the facts?

There is no possibility of proving a theory like this by logical reasoning. Even if we could be quite sure that some sort of system was used and that a part of that system involved the use of different calendars, there are always a number of possible alternatives, as regards the types of calendar, the starting-point of these calendars,[34] the calendar used for each event, etc. In this sense an element of arbitrariness must be involved in the choice. A definite answer can therefore be obtained only by testing the hypothesis.

The first proof of a theory is that it works. Stenring started by seeing if the chronological contradictions in the OT could be explained. Have they been explained?

Stenring's tables—from which an extract is given in Appendix 2—show the dates of the time-fixed events recorded in the Bible from the Creation to the Return from Captivity. These tables give both the number of days from the Creation to the event in question and the dates in the three calendars concerned—and in fact also tell us if the event took place on the boundary between two days, that is, at the sunset hour.

I have carried out sample checks on these calculations and have not found any errors. I compared the dates and the intervals of time with the information given in the Bible. I found no disagreement on any point with the exact wording in the text. *All the contradictions in the sections covered by the system seem to have been resolved.*

[34] E. Frank, *Talmudic and Rabbinical Chronology*, pp. 14-16. According to the rabbis, the beginning of the Jewish chronology may have started on the second, third, etc. day of Creation.

It hardly seems necessary to emphasize that this is a remarkable result. A theory which yields full agreement with the given facts, where other theories have failed, cannot be dismissed without strong counter-arguments.

There is, however, one question which must be answered before the value of this finding can be estimated. Is it not true to say that the system with these different calendars, which can be used alternatively, is so flexible that it is fairly easy to make it fit the given biblical dates?

It must be admitted that—at any rate theoretically—the system is very flexible. The calendars *could* be combined in many different ways. In the solution given there is, however, a certain logic and consistency, as has already been pointed out (page 8). But what in this connection is still more important is that the restrictions imposed by the solution are so severe. Everything has to agree with the chronological data in the Bible—year, season, date, day of the week and even hour of the day.

Tests on some events

These restrictions will be illustrated by a couple of examples. According to *one* statement (Gen. 5.32), Shem was 100 years old when Noah was 600 (in Gen. 7.11 it is stated that this was in the *same* year as the Deluge). According to *another* statement (Gen. 11.10), Shem was still 100 years old when his son Arpachshad was born, two years *after* the Deluge. According to Stenring, this contradiction is explained by the fact that in the first case it is a question of lunar years of 354 days, while in the second case Shem's age is measured in standard years of 365 days, with an extra intercalary day every fourth year. However, the interesting point is that Stenring's hypothesis requires that 100 years *to the day* shall elapse from the date (fixed by other chronological data) when Noah was 600 years old to the birth of Arpachshad, exactly two years after the end of the Deluge (the 27th day of the 2nd month; cf. Gen. 8.14). The random chance that such a solution will exist is not great. However, Stenring shows that this solution does exist. Within the framework of the system adopted, the birth of Arpachshad is linked with an exact date (the year, the month, the day and even the time of day), with respect to which there is no scope for arbitrariness.[35]

Furthermore, as regards the date of the destruction of Jerusalem,

---

[35] Stenring, op. cit., p. 89.

one of the calendars must indicate the 7th day of the 5th month (II Kings 25.8), while at the same time another must indicate the 10th day of the same month (Jer. 25.12). About 25 years later one calendar must indicate the 27th day of the 12th month as the date of the rehabilitation of Jehoiachin (II Kings 25.27), while another indicates the 25th day of the same month (Jer. 52.31). In an appendix to Stenring's book (see appendix 1) I have shown that it is possible to calculate the year and the day for these events purely mathematically, if we accept the "rules of the game" on which the system has been based.[36] The solution which emerges is in complete agreement with the conclusions which Stenring has arrived at in another way. Statistically there was only one chance in ten that *any* solution existed at all. The solution provides absolute datings for these two events, datings which are so exact that from a formal point of view the events must have occurred in the transitional period between two dates, i.e. during the hour of sunset. It can be shown that the direct conclusion from this is that all changes of ruler during the period of the divided kingdom took place at sunset, according to the formal system. In fact, in the two cases in which the text reports the time of day when a change of ruler took place (I Kings 23.35; II Kings 11.9), it is also mentioned that the respective ruler died at sunset.

The events surrounding the Exodus from Egypt may be taken as a third example. In this case there is an accumulation of different chronological data — ages, the date of Aaron's death, the period of wandering in the wilderness, the dates when the Israelites began to eat manna and when they stopped eating manna, etc. In my appendix 1, I have shown how these data lead to the conclusion that only one explanation of the exact time is possible for the whole complex of events, if the "rules of the game" are followed.[37] In this case there was an extremely small chance, from a statistical point of view, that there could be a solution which was in agreement — to the day — with all this chronological information from different biblical books. But nevertheless there was a solution.

Working in this way and testing all the possibilities of using different calendars, different alternatives given in the text, etc., it can be shown mathematically and statistically that, merely for these groups of events, the chance of finding a solution which satisfies the given

---

[36] Op. cit., p. 95.
[37] Op. cit., p. 90.

conditions is very small indeed, in fact only a fraction of a million. A solution has nevertheless emerged. The chances of adapting the system secondarily to the data given are so small that they must, for all practical purposes, be excluded. Thus, *the mathematical tests show with a high degree of certainty that the proposed chronology must have been applied in the shaping of these sections of the OT.*

These calculations are also of interest from another point of view. They show that for all specific events connected with the Deluge, the Exodus and the Captivity, the system admits of only one solution. *There is no place for arbitrariness.* Other chronological data, such as that the Temple was built in the 480th year after the Exodus or that Jephthah sent messages to the king of the children of Ammon 300 years after the Israelite settlement in the land east of Jordan (Judges 11.26), very quickly fix other key data. The scope for subjectively chosen solutions is very small, if any. The events are fixed to the year and the day, in fact, in most cases also to the time of the day.

Tests on series of events

The possibilities of alternative solutions can also be tested for long series of events, at any rate for certain parts of the chronology. Thus, I have achieved a purely mathematical solution for the period of the divided kingdom. It is well known that a great many solutions have been tried for this period. However, before Stenring nobody was able to present a chronology, which took satisfactory account of all the information given, especially in I and II Kings and I and II Chronicles. Every previous writer on this subject has been forced to suppose that some of the data given are wrong, because of the contradictions.

If, however, we leave aside other historical sources and just concentrate on the information given in the Bible, it is possible to handle the problem mathematically. In doing so, it may be supposed that the same type of year is used when the texts specify the lengths of the reigns of the different kings, the dates of their accessions in relation to the reign of the king in the neighbouring country, and so on. Furthermore it is supposed that co-regencies, but not interregnums, may occur. For the rest, the rules of the system are used.

With these restrictions it is possible to express the chronological information in equations, in which the unknown terms are the length of the co-regency and the reign of each separate king. We thus have a system which includes all the mathematical possibilities within the given frame. The system is complicated and the solution is not easy.[38] But it is possible. What sort of solution does the system give in this case?

It gives one solution, which is identical with that found by Stenring in a more reasoning way. This is also the single solution for the period from the division of the kingdom after Solomon's death to the day when the usurper Jehu seized power and killed the kings of Israel and Judah. It is also the single solution from the time of Hezekiah's death to the beginning of the Captivity (there may have been co-regencies not mentioned in the text, which are impossible to check from the OT itself, as for this period there are no parallel kings in Israel for comparison).

For the period from Jehu to Hezekiah's death the situation is a bit more complicated. It is theoretically possible that Joash of Judah reigned five years less than in the solution given by Stenring. However, this later solution has very strong support in some remarkable "coincidences", which I shall deal with later on. Thus, we may safely

---

[38] The construction of the equations can be elucidated by the following example, starting with the accession of Jehu after he had killed the kings of Israel and Judah. According to the Bible, Jehu reigned for 28 years ($= a_1$) and was succeeded by Jehoahaz, who reigned for 17 years. It is supposed that his eventual co-regency with his father lasted a_2 years, while the sole regency lasted a_3 years. So one alternative is that $a_2 + a_3 = 17$ (where a_2 and a_3 may also be 0), another that the information in the Bible only refers to his period as sole regent (i.e. $a_3 = 17$), in which case there is a possibility that he was also co-regent in addition (a_2 greater or equal to 0). Jehoahaz was succeeded by Jehoash, who reigned for 16 years. If a_4 is the period of co-regency and a_5 that of sole regency, obviously either $a_4 + a_5 = 16$ or $a_5 = 16$, in which case a_4 so far is indefinite. His contemporary in Judah, Athaliah, reigned for 6 years, whereafter her grandson Joash was put on the throne. Further Jehoash became king in the 37th year of Joash. The following alternative equations can then be stated:

Eq. 1 (Jehoahaz' regency)
   Alt. 1: $a_3 = 17$, a_2 indefinite
   Alt. 2: $a_2 + a_3 = 17$

Eq. 2 (Jehoash's regency)
   Alt. 1: $a_5 = 16$, a_4 indefinite
   Alt. 2: $a_4 + a_5 = 16$

Eq. 3 (synchronism)
   Alt. 1: $28 + a_3 = 6 + (36 \text{ to } 37)$
   Alt. 2: $28 + a_3 - a_4 = 6 + (36 \text{ to } 37)$

In Eq. 3, Alt. 1, the first term refers to Jehu's reign, the second to Jehoahaz' sole regency, and the third to Athaliah's regency, while the fourth indicates the 37th year. Alt. 1 thus relates to the case in which the information in II Kings 13.10 refers to Jehoash's accession as sole king. Alt. 2 relates to the case in which it means his accession as co-regent. In this way chains of alternative equations can be established. The whole system was complex but solvable.

conclude that the purely mathematical solution of this part of the chronology provides strong evidence that with the proposed system a formal solution of all the contradictions in this part of the Bible is possible and also that the given solution is the right one within the framework of the system.

CHAPTER FIVE

THE QUESTION OF RIGHT SEASONS

The proposed system is remarkable in its exactness and in the many angles from which it can be checked. Thus, it must agree with regard to the division into weekdays. For example, if the text states that the 7th day after manna began to fall was a Sabbath day (Ex. 16.30) or that Athaliah was killed when the men who were to act as guards on the Sabbath came on duty (II Kings 11.9), then the event must also fall on a Sabbath day, if we start reckoning the week from the beginning of the Creation. A check on Stenring's tables also shows that this is the case.

I have already mentioned that the solution often fixes the time of the day for an event. Of course, this must agree with the text when the time is given or hinted at. This is also the case, as far as as I can see.

The standard calendar shows the seasons

In this chapter I shall, however, discuss another check—a check on the season. The reason is that Stenring considers that one of the calendars used—the standard calendar of 365 days with an extra intercalated day every fourth year—was intended to show the right seasons, starting the new year in close connection with the vernal equinox, like the Jewish religious calendar of that time. This would also be in perfect agreement with the text of the Canopus Decree in 238 B.C.—the decree which established this type of calendar in Egypt. The text of the Decree emphasizes that with this calendar the seasons will come in their right places in relation to the festivals.

Stenring gives in his book three examples of correspondence between the season and the date in the standard calendar. The two events mentioned in Gen. 30.14 and I Sam. 6.13 happened, according to the text, in the days of the wheat harvest. Stenring's tables show the first and the last day in the third month respectively, i.e. the wheat harvest should have fallen around June. Furthermore in Num. 13.20-26 it is said that spies were sent out when the first grapes were ripe and returned 40 days later with an enormous cluster of grapes. In the tables this period falls between around 20 July and 1 September. Both the time of the wheat harvest and the time of ripe grapes agree very well with what is known of the harvest today and from ancient times.

However, Stenring also cites a text in which the season does not seem to agree with his tables. In Jos. 3.15, dealing with the crossing of the Jordan, it is said that "the feet of the priests that bare the ark were dipped in the brim of the water (for Jordan overfloweth all his banks all the time of harvest)". But in the tables the event falls in the last half of September, which normally is not called harvest time in the Bible. Stenring remarks, however, that the text never tells us explicitly that the crossing *is* at the time of harvest; it only puts two statements together which give this impression.[39] A somewhat cryptical way of writing can obviously also be a means of keeping the secret of the chronology.

The question of a season-bound calendar in the OT is very interesting and worth studying more closely. I have therefore gone through all the events recorded by Stenring in his tables, trying to find if something in the text points to a definite season. The result is rather interesting.

Tests of the Theory

Starting with the first book of the Bible, Gen. 41.54 speaks of the day when the years of plenty were ended and the years of dearth began. It is interesting to note how this day—fixed by the dates of other events—"happens" to fall in the standard calendar on the 1st day of the 3rd month, i.e. the month of the wheat harvest. We may say that it is very logical that the time of dearth should start on the day when the first bad harvest began.

Let us continue with the Exodus. It is supposed to have taken place on the 15th day of the 1st month, which means in April, if we suppose that the Jewish religious calendar started around 1 April. But does the Bible text give the impression that it was spring?

Shortly before the Exodus "hail smote throughout all the land of Egypt all that was in the field, both man and beast; and the hail smote every herb of the field and brake every tree of the field" (Ex. 9.25).

---

[39] This idea is even more pronounced in the Septuagint: "And the feet of the priests, who were carrying the ark of the covenant of the Lord, were dipped into a part of the water of the Jordan, though the Jordan overflowed all its banks, *as* in the days of wheat harvest". The drying up of the Jordan is normally explained as a consequence of an earthslip, which dammed up the river, probably because of heavy rain. According to Stenring's tables, the event took place at the end of September or the beginning of October when such heavy rains are quite possible.

"And the flax and the barley were smitten: for the barley was in the ear, and the flax was in bud. But the wheat and the rye were not smitten: for they were not grown up" (Ex. 9.31).

In what season of the year could there have been so much difference in development between the different crops that barley was in the ear but the wheat was not grown up and was therefore undamaged by a hail that smote every herb of the field and was followed by a fire running along the ground? In fact, hardly any, if we are concerned with one-crop cultivation. In those days barley and wheat were normally sown at about the same time, after the Nile floods had withdrawn but before the ground had dried out.[40] This concentration in sowing caused by the Nile floods—normally in November and at the beginning of December—corresponded to a rather concentrated harvest of wheat and barley in April and the beginning of May.[41] The difference in development mentioned in the text is therefore unlikely. It is also very unlikely that the wheat, close to Easter, should hardly have come up out of the ground but nonetheless should be ready for harvesting at the beginning of May.

There is, however, an explanation. At the beginning of the third century B.C. Ptolemy II worked hard to introduce two-crop cultivation on the fertile land irrigated from the canals and for this purpose much work was done to adapt the canal and irrigation system to the new method.[42] In the middle of the century great tracts of land round Alexandria and Faijum were cultivated in this way.[43] One main form of two-crop cultivation was to sow barley in the summer and after the harvest to sow winter wheat at the normal time.

This system corresponds well to the season, as given in Stenring's tables. According to these tables, the Exodus fell on the 15th day of the 1st month in the solar calendar. But the standard calendar then shows the 3rd day of the 6th month, i.e. around *the beginning of September.*

In fact, almost everything in the account of the plagues of Egypt points to some time around late summer and early autumn. Even the

---

[40] M. Schnebel, *Die Landwirtschaft im hellenistischen Ägypten* (1925).
[41] Op. cit., p. 162.
[42] Op. cit. and H. Kees, Ägypten (*Handbuch der Altertumswissenschaft* 3 : 1).
[43] This is verified by a papyrus concerning the distribution of seed from the state supplies. Also Diodorus, visiting Egypt in the year 59 B.C., tells how the delta land around Alexandria was traversed by systems of canals, from which the surrounding land was irrigated by Archimedes' "screw" (Book 1.34).

first plague—discoloured, stinking water—gives this impression.[44] In the second plague Aaron stretched out his hand over the streams, the rivers and the ponds of Egypt and the frogs came up and covered the land. In the late winter and early spring, the Nile withdraws and the canals and the ponds dry out. This is no time for an invasion of frogs. In August-September, however, the flood is at its high point and in some years all the watercourses have an abundance of frogs.

The third and the fourth plagues (lice or gnats and flies) are also improbable in the late winter but are very common under the warm, flooded conditions in August-September. Also the fifth and the sixth plagues (murrain, boils and blains) may develop rapidly under the same conditions. What is said about the eighth plague is also interesting. One day a strong *east* wind blew, which brought the locusts, which ate all the *fruit* of the trees. Summer and autumn are the seasons for fruit in Egypt. The period August-September also agrees well with the behaviour of the locusts. It is generally supposed that by locusts a species of *Schistocerca gregaria* is meant. This species swarms in *warm weather* and is often carried by the wind for very great distances. Normally these locusts dwell in the highlands of Iran during the *late summer and early autumn* and can be carried from there to Egypt by strong east winds.[45]

As the circumstances of the plagues have been described very realistically, it would be strange if a season (late winter to early spring) had been chosen which was impossible in all respects. But the period given by Stenring (August-September) suits the text perfectly.

In the Wandering in the Wilderness we have two events of interest in this connection. Ex. 16.13 and Num. 11.13 tell how the people on two occasions were fed with quails, which covered the camp and were brought in by the wind from the sea. This is a quite natural phenomenon, when the quails are gathered to migrate. Thus, Brehm tells[46] us how on the African coast one can see the quails coming in like clouds and then immediately falling down on the shore and lying as if dead, especially when they have had to fight against strong winds. The only season when things like this can happen in a natural way is, however, during the migration of the birds. Otherwise quails never fly in big flocks. The birds generally arrive in this part of the world at the

---

[44] This discolouring has often been explained as being due to slime caused by the inundation (which normally reaches its peak in August-September).

[45] Brehm, *Tierleben*.

[46] Op. cit.

beginning of October and leave in April-May. From Stenring's tables it is possible to calculate that the first event happened at the beginning of October and the second in the latter half of May. Thus, both events fell in that limited time of the year when a natural explanation was possible.

Judges 3.20 tells us that Eglon was sitting in his *summer* parlour, when Ehud thrust the dagger into his belly. According to the standard calendar, this event happened at the beginning of August.

In Judges 6.3 is said that, *when Israel had sown*, the Midianites used to come up and encamp against them and destroy the increase of the earth. It is also natural to think that the Midianite nomads brought in their herds at the beginning of the growing period, let them pasture on the fields and stayed over harvest, taking as much as possible from the crop. It is also related that Gideon was called when he was threshing wheat in his wine press, to hide it from the Midianites. He was called just when the Midianites had, as usual, crossed the river and pitched their tents in the valley of Jezreel (it must have been some time after the sowing). Therefore he was not threshing from the new crop. In the hot and dry harvest time, such a heavy fall of dew as is mentioned in 6.38 would also have been improbable. Stenring gives the period January-February for this event, which agrees well both with the dew and with the fact that the sowing time normally varied between the middle of November and the middle of January.[47]

Judges 9.27 tells how the men of Shechem gathered their grapes from the vineyards and trod the grapes and made merry. This was the beginning of a series of events lasting 2-3 months, as far as can be seen from the text, a series of events which ended in the death of Abimelech. For this the standard calendar gives the 28th day of the 6th month, i.e. around September-October. Obviously the agreement is good in this case also.

Of the following time-fixed events, I cannot find more than two which give some indication of the season. One is the story told in Jer. 36.22 of how king Jehoiakim burned Jeremiah's scroll in the brazier burning before him in the *winter* house. According to the standard calendar, this would have happened on the 28th-30th day of the 9th month i.e. December-January.[48]

---

[47] Albright, The Gezer Calendar, *Bull. of the American Schools of Oriental Research*, no. 92.

[48] One puzzling thing in this narrative is that Jer. 36.1 tells that Jeremiah wrote down his prophecies in the *4th* year of the reign of king Jehoiakim, but that Jer. 36.9 says

Jer. 36.30 also gives a hint as to the season. According to the text, the dead body of Jehoiakim was to be cast out in the day to the heat, and in the night to the frost. These changes in temperature point to winter time or early spring. The standard calendar gives about the middle of January for Jehoiakim's death.

Stenring has not commented on these agreements and seems only to have been aware of those mentioned on page 25. Of course, some of them may be due to chance. However, to me it seems almost impossible to get such an agreement in *all* the cases studied, if the proposed system is essentially unsound. The designers of the system must have gone to work with the utmost care also in details concerning the seasons and must have had a good knowledge of the characteristics of the different periods of the year. Certainly some of the information about the seasons—as, for example, in Ex. 9.31-32—was directly inserted by the redactors.

---

that it was not read in public before the *5th*, in the 9th month. In the meantime Nebuchadnezzar, according to the Babylonian cuneiform tablets, conquered Syria and Judah. But if the purpose of Jeremiah was to *warn* the people and so avoid the evil, why was he silent for more than a year at the most decisive time? With help of Stenring's tables it is possible to arrive at an explanation (Stenring himself has not commented on this point). The 4th year is according to the standard calendar, the 5th according to the lunar one. The three first days of the 5th year in the lunar calendar coincide with the last days of the 9th month in the 4th year in the standard calendar. To fix an event at a definite time with the aid of such methods is very typical of the chronological system of the OT.

CHAPTER SIX

THE CONCEALED MEANINGS OF DATES

A good chronological system has a value in itself. To bring order into what was previously disorder, to fix every important event in its right place is of the utmost importance in historical writing and thus also in religious historical writing. This is especially true when the writing is the text of sacred books and when chronology, as such, is closely connected with religion and is almost sacred itself. So we can be certain that just to establish a chronology was a sufficient goal for the biblical redactors.

But, in addition, it must have been very tempting for the designers of the system to give a deeper significance (some hidden meaning) to some important dates and periods of time. The whole age was soaked in ideas about the symbolism of numbers and the significance of dates (especially of religious festivals)—good dates and bad dates for doing important things—and of the connections between the heavenly bodies, the reckoning of time and the fate of man.

In the Book of Jubilees—written perhaps in the second century B.C.—we find very interesting examples of this. Primarily, all the events from the Creation to the Exodus are arranged in their chronological order within the framework of the jubilees, i.e. the periods of seven sabbatical years or 49 years. But secondarily, most important events—especially if they have a religious content—are placed on certain calendar dates, such as New Year's Day, new-month days and, above all, the Feast of Weeks, which, according to the jubilee calendar, was celebrated on the 15th day of the 3rd month.[49] This was the most important feast for the Jewish circles in which the Book of Jubilees was written and was especially connected with the different covenants between God and His people. To place an event on a "good" date obviously increased its importance.

Such things are only to be expected in the biblical chronology. On

---

[49] The events which, according to the Book of Jubilees, fell on the 15th day of the 3rd month have been enumerated by Morgenstern in *Vet. Test.*, 1955, p. 56. In the Book of Jubilees, in which the central motif is the necessity of keeping the laws and regulations prescribed in the different covenants, the emphasis on the Feast of the Covenant is also natural.

the other hand, we cannot expect them to the same extent as in the Book of Jubilees. There it was an easy task to place an event on a certain date. In the biblical chronology it is not. We have already seen how many restrictions there were and how strictly the different dates were fixed. Even for the designers of the system it must therefore in most cases have been difficult to place a single event on an "interesting" date.

However, there is a definite tendency in this direction, in fact, to a remarkable extent. I cannot here give an account of all the proofs, but will try to give the most important examples. Most of them have been pointed out by Stenring, but I found also others. Probably there are even more to be found. To make it easier for the reader to check the examples, I mostly give the number of the event in question in brackets. The numbers refer to the tables given in Appendix 2, which may be consulted to check what follows.

Connections with New Year's Day

In the same way as in the Book of Jubilees, there are thus connections with New Year's Day. The divided kingdom proves to have begun on the first day of the year (177), which is significant, as this was a quite new period in the history of Israel and New Year's Day symbolizes the beginning. In connection with this, it may be mentioned that also the next event (178) — Jeroboam's feast — certainly took place on the 15th day of the 8th month in one calendar, as the text states. But in another calendar this day turns out to have been the first day of the year in question. In reality it was thus a New Year feast.[50] In other respects associations with the first day of the year may occur both as regards "historical" events, such as the death of Terah (58), the marriage of Esau (65, which in fact has two dates in common with 58), the establishment of the Tabernacle in the wilderness, etc., and as regards prophetic visions, such as Ezekiel's vision of the new Temple (287) and his last great prophecy (290).

Sometimes the event not only falls on New Year's Day but also

[50] It is often supposed that Jeroboam did not really sacrifice to two calves at this feast (I Kings 12.32), but that these "calves" were just the foundation of the invisible Jahwe. Considering that this is a New Year feast and considering the very active role of the king himself, sacrificing at the altar, the feast seems to come very close to the accession feast, which Mowinckel (*Psalmenstudien*) argues was celebrated in Jerusalem every New Year (cf. I Kings 12.32: "like unto the feast that is in Judah"). At this feast the accession of Jahwe and the accession of the king are supposed to have been celebrated in a cultic drama, in much the same way as in Babylon.

coincides with the first day of a new century. This is true of the celebration of the Feast of Tabernacles for the first time after the Exile (300), which at one time seems to have been the starting-point for the post-exilic life of Israel and the end-point of the chronological system of the OT. This event was assigned, as it should be, to the 7th month and should, by the law, have taken place on the 15th day. This is also the case in the lunar calendar. But in the solar calendar this is the date when 3,300 solar years had elapsed since the Creation. This is unquestionably an effective, although a well-concealed conclusion to the chain of events.

Another example is (234). When Hezekiah, after the cleansing of the Temple, takes the remarkable step of postponing the celebration of the Passover for a month (II Chron. 30), the celebration "happens" to coincide exactly too the hour with the beginning of the year 3100 after the Creation, according to the standard calendar (the evening of 14.2.3102 in the solar calendar coincides with the evening of 5.13.3099—i.e. the beginning of a new century—according to the standard calendar).

Connections with the Passover

Perhaps even more illustrative than the connections with New Year's Day is the association with the Feast of the Passover—a direct parallel to the Feast of Weeks in the Book of Jubilees. On the one hand, there are all the open accounts of the celebration of the Passover and, on the other, the concealed accounts. There seems to be one such account even in Gen. 6.1. If we count 120 lunar years backwards from the day when the Deluge covered the mountain tops and the first human race disappeared, we arrive, according to the tables, at the beginning of the Passover (the 14th day of the 1st month) in the standard calendar and at the end of the Passover celebrations (the 21st day of the 1st month) in the solar calendar. This unique calendar situation with the whole Passover feast contained in one date is scarcely due to chance but seems to have been deliberately chosen. A similar double association proves to underlie the date of Ezekiel's grandiose vision of his calling (262). The date given in the text (the 5th day of the 4th month) turns out to fall in the two other calendars on the day of the Passover and on the first day of the *massot* festival, respectively.

All the concealed associations with the celebration of the Passover will not be reported in detail here. However, it scarcely seems to be due to chance that the first High Priest, Aaron, was born on the 14th day of the 1st month (90) or that on the same date Samuel sacrificed a suckling lamb, a sacrifice which ushered in the termination of Israel's 40 years of servitude to the Philistines and thereby marked the commencement of the period of kingly rule (161). In a similar way, increased importance is given to the division of Canaan between the twelve tribes of Israel (136) by the fact that the event falls on the date of the Passover.

I have already mentioned how additional chronological effect and thereby additional sanctity and weight was given to Hezekiah's celebration of the Passover by postponing the celebration for a month. It is interesting to note that this particular Passover celebration, which is not mentioned in the Books of Kings but has three chapters devoted to it in the Books of Chronicles, is taken as the starting-point in further securing the privileges and rights attached to the priesthood in Jerusalem. The Feast of the Passover stands out as a feast of God's covenant and promise. But its character as a sacrificial feast makes it, at the same time, an exceptional means of strengthening the position of the Temple and the Temple priests. This aspect appears to have been of no interest to the author of the Book of Jubilees, and his chronological perspective has changed, perhaps in deliberate opposition to the official Judaism of the priests.

Equal dates

There are also "coincidences" not connected with festivals. Sometimes it may seem like a game with figures, behind which, however, a deeper meaning is certainly concealed, according to the contemporary view. The progenitor of mankind (Adam) and the progenitor of the new generation of man (Noah) have been connected in a symbolic way by a common date, the same date of death in the standard calendar, which is a noteworthy coincidence if due to chance (11 and 50). Something similar happens in the case of Enoch, who was born and died on the same date in both the lunar calendar (the 7th day of the 1st month) and in the solar calendar (the 10th day of the 4th month) (see (8) and (12)). His life unites, so to speak, the lunar and the solar chronologies and fixes the mutual relations of the calendars. As we know, his lifetime (365 years) makes a direct reference to the 365 days of a solar year. In the pseudepigraphic literature—especially in the Book of Enoch—Enoch is also given an exceptional position, as the man who knows and explains the secrets of the heavenly bodies and of chronology.

The foundation of the new generation of man after the Deluge is especially marked. Thus, the date of Arpachshad's birth (38) falls on the same day in the lunar and solar calendars (the 11th day of the 3rd month), a date which is further emphasized by the fact that the next decisive event—Abraham's departure (51)—also takes place on the same date in both calendars (there is statistically only one chance in about 360 that dates from different calendars will coincide at all). To return to Arpachshad, his birthday coincides in two calendars with that of his grandson Eber (40). As we have already seen (page 7) Arpachshad's birth was one of the striking "contradictions" resolved by Stenring and this solution also definitely determined the date of the birth. So we must say that the designers of the system have really used Arpachshad as a reference point.

Another example of a reference point is event 192, which in fact comprises six events, including the deaths of two kings and the accessions of four kings. It is interesting to note that this point is placed exactly where the solar calendar has gone two revolutions more than the standard year and the dates again are the same in both the calendars. It is as if the designers, after having built the road so far, felt the need to gather up the different narrative lines and set up a mile-stone. Such "double dates" are also used for many other events in the chronology.

Equal dates can also be used to mark internal connections. To take an example from the Book of Ezekiel, the prophet's prediction of the destruction of the Temple (Ez. 20.1; 23.47), the actual destruction of the Temple and finally the prophet's vision of the new Temple (events 269, 283 and 287) prove to fall on the same date (the 10th day of the 5th month) but in three different calendars.

Another example is the carrying away of Jehoiachin after the first conquest of Jerusalem (260), which proves to have two dates in common (7/5, 18/2) with Zedekiah's carrying away after the second conquest (283). Such occurrences would, of course, be remarkable if they were due to chance. Examples of this type may be multiplied.

The dates of Ezekiel

In some of the books the years and dates seem to be especially stressed. The Book of Ezekiel gives such an example. Many dates are given in connection with the prophecies. But they are surprisingly isolated from the rest of the text, their significance is difficult to see and they are often vague and difficult to interpret. In Stenring's analysis, however, the disorder and meaninglessness turn out to have some sort of order and meaning. The obscure and much debated expression in 1.1 ("in the thirtieth year")[51] proves to be calculated from the important religious reform of Josiah. The likewise obscure expressions in 4.4-6 about 390 and 40 days and years[52] turns out to mean exactly 430 years to the day from the date when Jerusalem was made the capital by David. We have already seen how the vision in which Ezekiel was called is directly connected by the date with two main festivals in Israel, how two other visions are connected with New Year's Day and how the prophecy about the destruction of the Temple is connected both with the actual destruction and with the vision of the new Temple. More than half of the prophecies occur on the first day of the month in one calendar or another. This fact may be compared with Ezekiel's great interest in the New Year and new-month sacrifices, for which he prescribed new rules, which in part conflicted with the law of Moses. Things like the use of "double dates" may also be mentioned, as well as the placing of the day when the king of Babylon laid siege to Jerusalem on the first of the epagomenal days in the normal Egyptian solar calendar—in the Egyptian view, a potentially unlucky day, when nothing should be done. It is also possible to trace a certain periodicity concerning the dated occasions on which the Lord spoke to Ezekiel. After his wife's death in the evening of the day after event no. 272 (the change between the dates 11.10 and 12.10.), exactly one "year of mourning" elapses before Ezekiel again receives a prophecy (274). Seven weeks after this comes the next prophecy (276), and then no. 277 and no. 278

---

[51] It had been supposed that the time was reckoned from the accession of Manasseh (Torrey) or Nabopolassar (Eichhorn, König, etc.), the fall of Samaria (Smith), the birth of the prophet (Kraetzschmar, Irwin, etc.), a year of jubilee (Fisch) and also the reform of Josiah (Hieronymus, Hävernick, Broegelmann, Ziegler). Stenring thus demonstrates that the last explanation is the right one.

[52] Earlier explanations (cf. Ziegler, Fisch, etc.) have been that the 40 years were the period for which the present generation of the tribe of Judah had to be punished in captivity, that the 390 years were the period between the division of the kingdom and the fall of Jerusalem or from the building of the Temple to its destruction. Other scholars point to the period mentioned in the Septuagint (190 years) and try to fit it in between the fall of Samaria and the edict of Cyrus. A parallel has also been drawn between the total of 430 years of misdeeds and the period which the people of Israel spent in Egypt (Ex. 12.40). The 40 years for Judah also have a striking parallel in Num. 14.33-34.

follow at even two-week intervals. There are likewise two weeks between no. 280 and no. 281. The same period has previously elapsed between no. 262 and no. 263. Possibly these systematic intervals indicate a definite scheme of preparation before the contact with the Deity. In the later Jewish throne-chariot mysticism we find the use of periods for ascetic exercises—lasting in some cases 12 days and in others 14 days—before the visionary feels himself raised up to the seven heavenly mansions.[53]

I will not tire the reader with more examples. Bearing in mind the fact that most of the dates are definitely fixed by other restrictions given in the biblical text, all these "coincidences" would be quite incredible if they were only due to chance. It was also very natural to use the system for creating a special meaning in some dates. As the example of the Book of Jubilees shows, such methods were also used in other respects.

Are Sabbath days avoided?

Was an effort made not only to place events on certain days but also to avoid events falling on other days, such as the Sabbath? In the Book of Jubilees this effort is strongly marked. No event falls on a Sabbath day, which is understandable if we think of the stress which was laid on keeping the Sabbath holy. It was very easy to avoid such a thing with the type of chronology used in this book.

In the chronological system of the OT—which is subject to so many other restrictions—it was considerably more difficult, in fact, almost impossible, to avoid events falling on a Sabbath day. Keeping the Sabbath does not play such a predominant role in the OT as it does in the Book of Jubilees. Stenring has not discussed this question and does not seem to think that such a purpose was part of the system.

Nevertheless I have investigated whether any events really are placed on Sabbath days. According to the tables, a few events fall on the Sabbath, but to me these events seem questionable. One is number 119—the sending out of the spies. Stenring does not fix the time of the day in this case. As far as I can see, there is nothing in the text to fix the hour. In that case we could very well assume that the spies were sent out at sunset. To send out a patrol protected by the falling darkness at the beginning of a new week is in fact to choose a very suitable time.

---

[53] Scholem, *Major Trends in Jewish Mysticism* (1948).

Another is 132—the crossing of the Jordan. According to the text, the people came up out of Jordan on the 10th day of the 1st month, which turns out to be a Sabbath day. Jos. 2 tells that two men were sent out to spy. If they were sent out on the very evening when the days of weeping and mourning for Moses were ended, the relation in the text agrees very well with the timetable for the actual crossing on the 9th day and the gathering on the opposite side just when the Sabbath was beginning on the 10th. This manner of placing the events as far as possible at the sunset hour—when the day changes—is very typical of the whole system.

In the case of events 150 and 169 Stenring does not fix the time of the day. As far as I can see, nothing in the text or in the general design prevents these events being placed in the evening. About events 171 and 172 I have a different opinion from Stenring, who places the events in the morning. It seems to me that placing them in the evening before is more in agreement with I Kings 8.65.

Besides these events, only nos. 152, 154, 267 and 281 fall on Sabbath days. These events are of such a nature that they may very well be allowed to fall on the Sabbath. Nothing in the text seems to preclude them taking place in the evening, with the possible exception of 267.

If these explanations are correct, we have the same situation in the chronological system as in the Book of Jubilees, i.e. no events fall on the Sabbath. Personally, I think that it was meant to be so but at the same time I admit that this is difficult to prove, because so many of the events fall at the sunset hour. Perhaps one of the reasons for this was that only with such a design was it possible to avoid the fatal combination of the Sabbath with the event?

CHAPTER SEVEN

PERIODS IN THE SYSTEM

In Chapter VI we found that in the chronological system a special meaning was given to certain dates. In this chapter I shall discuss the use — concealed or open — of certain periods. The use of such periods is by no means peculiar to the Bible and therefore it may also be of interest to compare the Bible with other antique writings in this respect.

Periods of 40 years or days

The use of the number 40 in connection with periods of time is especially obvious in the Bible. Thus, from the time of Moses to that of Solomon various periods of 40 years or days are mentioned (all periods, according to Stenring, are exact to the day). Moses fled from Egypt "when he was grown" (in Acts 7.23 the precise age of 40 years is given), met Pharaoh before the Exodus at the age of 80 years and died at the age of 120 years. Aaron also died 40 years after he met Pharaoh. Before the Exodus the children of Israel had been afflicted for 10 × 40 years in Egypt. Moses met God on Horeb and stayed there on several occasions for 40 days, Israel received manna for 40 years and spies were sent to Canaan for 40 days (one of them — Caleb — was 40 years of age). Because of the murmuring of the children of Israel against God, they were condemned to wander in the wilderness for 40 years. After Moses and Joshua, Israel was led by Othniel for 40 years, by Ehud and Shamgar for 2 × 40 years, by Barak for 40 years and by Gideon for 40 years. The period of Jair and the oppression by the children of Ammon lasted altogether 40 years, Eli was judge for 40 years and Israel was oppressed by the Philistines for 40 years. After Saul, his son Ish-bosheth was king at the age of 40 but was followed by David, who reigned for 40 years, and by Solomon, who also reigned for 40 years. The building of the Temple began in the 480th (12 × 40) year after the Exodus. All this information is directly given in the text. Stenring's analysis shows that Israel broke camp from Kadesh 40 weeks after the return of the spies, and later held the first Passover in the new country 40 days after Moses' death. Aaron's meeting with Pharaoh is not only 40 years before his death but also 6 × 40 years after the birth of Joseph. Analysis of certain other periods, such as the Deluge, also shows the frequency of periods of 40 years or days.

Among others, Hirzel[54] has pointed out the parallels in Greek and Hellenistic writing. Even Hesiod gives 40 years as the age of the mature man (compare the expression about Moses, "when he was grown", the age of Ish-bosheth when he was king, Caleb when he went on his dangerous task, the age of Isaac when he married Rebekah and the age of Esau when he married Judith). The famous Hellenistic chronologist Apollodorus also uses this method. Starting from the time when a poet, statesman, etc. "flourished", his birth is placed 40 years before.

Apollodorus and other writers also use the 40-year period for the length of a man's life-work. Here we find a strong Pythagorean tradition. According to this tradition, Pythagoras himself was 40 years old when he moved to Italy and there started his school[55] of philosophy and directed it until his death at 80 years of age. Especially in this sense there are many parallels in the Bible (the reigns of David and Solomon, the works of Moses and Aaron, the judges etc.). Also the period 3×40 years for a very great age is often found in antique writing. We may compare this with the age of Moses and also with Gen. 6.1, where the period of 120 years is given as a limit for the age of man before the Deluge.

There are parallels also for longer periods. Thus, the 480 years from the Exodus to the building of the Temple can be divided into 24 periods (18 leaders, judges and kings and 6 periods of oppression between them). The Greek historian Diodorus says of the Macedonian kings (Book VII): "From Caranus, who was the first to unite the power of Macedon and to hold it, to Alexander, who subdued the land of Asia, there are reckoned twenty-four kings and four hundred and eighty years".

Diodorus probably got his information from "the father of chronography", Eratosthenes, who was in charge of the library of Alexandria when the biblical chronology was probably constructed. It is likely that also Eratosthenes made much use of 40-year periods when he constructed the Greek chronology from Troy onwards.[56] Of

[54] R. Hirzel, Über Rundzahlen, *Sächs. Gesellsch. der Wissensch.* (1885).

[55] In the same way it is related of Plato that he was 40 years old on his first arrival at Syracuse.

[56] Apollodorus and probably Eratosthenes reckoned, for example, 80 years from the fall of Troy to the return of the Heraclids and 240 years from Troy to the flourishing of Homer.

a certain interest is also the fact that the representative of the last generation before the Exodus—Amram—died in the year 2400, according to Stenring's tables.

Other round periods than those based on 40 years were in use in the Bible, for example, periods of 70 years (the Captivity etc.) or 70 days. Other periods may also have played some part. Herodotus and some other Greek writers reckon 100 years for three generations (sometimes 33 years for one generation).[57] It may be noted that the beginning of the Exile, according to Stenring, fell in the middle of the year 3333 (lunar calendar) and that the biblical chronology *in toto* spans a period of exactly 3300 years (solar calendar).

Certainly it may also have some significance that the period of the divided kingdom (as Stenring points out) shows a pattern of 40 rulers in all (20 in Israel and 20 in Judah), distributed over 70 intervals of time, where the interval is determined by the birth of the ruler, his accession to the joint throne, his accession as sole ruler and his death or deposition. Even though this part of the OT was essentially based on historical material, there was always some possibility of the redactors achieving "interesting" figures by deciding how to deal with co-regencies and with rebels like Tibni, who ruled for one week, or Shallum, who ruled for one month.

However, I want to stress particularly the periods of 40 years or days, because of the great similarity between the Greeks and the Jews in other connections than chronology. The Greek woman was not allowed to visit the temple until 40 days after the birth of a boy (Censorin 11.7). We find the same rule in Lev. 12.2-4. Hirzel discusses the obvious parallels but cannot find any links between them and is apt to explain the magic significance of the figure 40 as something that developed independently amongst both Greeks and Jews. Others have claimed that the magic significance of 40 was of Semitic origin. But in fact it is difficult to find examples of the use of the figure 40 among other Semitic people before the time of Christ.[58] The Babylonians used 60 in a similar way and also gave it the same

[57] Book II, 142.
[58] W. H. Roscher (Die Zahl 40 im Glauben, Brauch und Schrifttum der Semiten, *K. Sächs. Ges. Wissensch.*, 1909) thus argues that this 40-year period is of Semitic origin. The proofs taken from the Assyrian-Babylonian culture are, however, very meagre indeed. As regards the Arabs, there seem to be no proofs before the time of Mohammed, after which the use of periods of 40 is abundant, probably because of Jewish influence. If this use of 40 is not derived from the Semitic sphere, its strong position in the OT seems very interesting.

meaning of indefinite magnitude which 40 had among the Greeks and the Jews.

If the biblical chronology was constructed in Hellenistic times, then there is always a possibility that the use of 40 in the Bible was just a loan. As has already been mentioned, the number 40 was in especial use among the Pythagoreans and had great significance in their number mystique. Pythagoras himself not only started his life-work in the age of 40 and thereafter worked for 40 years, according to the tradition, but is also said to have died after a 40-day fast, surrounded by his 40 closest disciples. Both Moses (Ex. 34.28) and Elijah (I Kings 19.8) used 40-day fasts. Lévy, among others, has pointed out series of similarities in the pseudepigraphic tales about Moses and the tales about Pythagoras and has also shown how strong the Pythagorean influence, as such, was in the apocryphal, pseudepigraphic and Talmudic writings, as well as in Jewish-Pharisaic views and rules.[59] This influence probably spread from the strong Jewish colony in Alexandria—the capital of the Hellenistic world.

It is, of course, difficult to elucidate at this stage, from where the Jews derived the mystical number 40. But it is worth considering whether it was not a result of Hellenistic influence.

Periods of jubilees

Before we leave the question of periods, I wish to mention briefly the periods of the jubilees. In the Book of Jubilees these periods are the framework of the whole system. In the OT we see less of them, but, according to Stenring, such periods are also part of the biblical system. In this case they are—as prescribed in the Law—reckoned as 50 years, not as 49 years, as in the Book of Jubilees. The first jubilee year must, of course, be supposed to have fallen some time after Moses received the Tables of the Law and the children of Israel settled in Canaan. The text seems to indicate that, according to the formal reckoning, the year when Israel crossed the Jordan was a year of rest (cf. Lev. 25.2). The first jubilee year falls three sabbatical periods later, according to Stenring.[60] It was the year after Israel had been rescued

---

[59] I. Lévy, *La légende de Pythagore de Grèce en Palestine* (1926).

[60] This was also the first possibility, according to the chronological system. One Sabbatical period after the crossing of Jordan, the land had just been divided among the tribes (event 136) and the rules for a jubilee year could not be put into use. Two periods after, the land was oppressed by the Mesopotamians.

by Othniel, who was then able to proclaim a year of jubilee, in order to restore the land to its proper owners (cf. Lev. 25.13), after it had been taken by the Mesopotamians. The Exile began 16 jubilee periods (800 years) later and 24 periods (1200 years) later came the first jubilee year after the chronological system had been constructed.[61] Probably these years were never observed but were used as part of the chronological system. In the above-mentioned two main periods we find a new connection with the number 40 as well as with the number 12.

All these periods, as well as the dates dealt with in Chapter VI, give some idea of the aims pursued in those parts of the OT that are connected with the chronology—let us call them C, by analogy with J, E and P. Perhaps some of these connections are just due to chance and are of no importance, but, in my opinion, most of them are significant. Difficult as it is now to get at all the ideas behind the system, there are probably more hidden meanings than have yet been revealed. They may be compared to an iceberg: the small part is visible, but the greater part remains hidden.

---

[61] This division of the time in simple proportions, such as 800/1200 = 2/3, is typical of the classical world (cf. J. Meysing, L'énigme de la chronologie biblique et qumrânienne dans une nouvelle lumière (*Revue de Qumran* 1967, p. 233)).

CHAPTER EIGHT

THE SYSTEM AND THE HISTORY

I have tried to test the chronological system from different points of view: how its principles agree with the background of time, whether it gives an explanation of biblical "contradictions", how well it stands up to mathematical tests, whether the seasons found agree with the text, if there are any remarkable connections with feasts, certain dates, even periods, etc. But there is another test that is of interest: does the chronology obtained agree in some way with the true chronology of history?

In one way this is not a real test. It may very well be that the biblical chronology has been restored to what it was meant to be, but that at the same time it agrees very badly with the real history. Nobody knows how good the sources of C really were. If C was designed several hundred years later than the events described really happened, then bad mistakes in chronology may well have been made. We have too many examples of this in other chronicles from other parts of the world.

Anyhow, let us try! The first problem is to connect the biblical system with some known point in factual history. We shall probably obtain the best connection if we choose some relatively late point, let us say, the beginning of Cyrus's first year in Babylon, which is event 296 in the system and according to secular history fell in the year 539-538 B.C.

There is, however, a restriction to be satisfied. The seven-day week has run from the time of C to the present day. One of the calendars used—the solar calendar—was in practical use in Egypt and we know on which weekday a certain date fell. According to Stenring, event 296 fell 1,204,484 days from the Creation (see Appendix). If we divide by seven, we find that the event was supposed to fall at the beginning of the third day of the week, which would at the same time be the 25th day of the 3rd month in the (civil) Egyptian solar calendar, as will be seen in the Appendix. This coincidence happens only once every seven years. Thus, it happened in the years 545, 538 and 531 B.C.[62]

---

[62] In the chronological system the dates are reckoned from the evening to the next evening; in the real Egyptian calendar the days were reckoned from the morning to the

As the real date of such an important event was probably approximately known, we may conclude that most likely event 296 was placed according to the middle alternative. This is, of course, a hypothesis, but we shall see what happens if we proceed further on this basis.

THE PERIOD OF THE DIVIDED KINGDOM

Firstly, I shall study the period around the Exile. In Table 1 the dates are shown of important events according to Stenring's tables and according to the Babylonian records.

Table 1
Comparative dates in the period 610-537 B.C.

Event	According to Stenring	According to the Babylonian records
Death of Josiah at the battle of Megiddo	610	609
Battle of Charchemish		605
Actual accession of Nebuchadnezzar		605
Jehoiakim carried off, beginning of Captivity	606-605	
Nebuchadnezzar's formal accession		604
First fall of Jerusalem	598	597
Second fall of Jerusalem	587	
Formal accession of Evil-Merodach	562	561
Formal accession of Cyrus	538	538
The first burnt offering of the returned Jews (Ezra 3.6)	537	537

The last event is, of course, not mentioned in the Babylonian records, but the probable date has been reckoned from the date of Cyrus's edict.[63]

Considering the schematical nature of the biblical chronology and the time that elapsed between the actual events and the period of C,

---

next morning. It is here supposed that the date in the system coincided with the real date, starting the next morning. Stenring has supposed that the date in the system coincided with the real date, starting *before* the evening, and therefore places event 296 in the year 539 B.C. However, the former solution seems more natural, gives a better agreement with the historical years and gives especially complete agreement between the sabbatical years in the system and the sabbatical years according to historical sources (cf. p. 54).

[63] For further comments on Table 1, see my article entitled "When did the Babylonian captivity begin?" (*Journ. of Theol. Stud.* 1967).

the dates agree remarkably well. It must be remembered that Stenring's dates are the result of a strict construction exclusively based on the chronological information given in the Bible. The only reference to secular history is the fitting with the aid of the seven-day week.

Special significance must be given to the beginning of the 70-year Captivity. A puzzling fact is that this did not last for 70 years at all, if the period is calculated in the normal way from the first or second fall of Jerusalem. But from Stenring's reconstruction it is obvious that the Captivity must be reckoned from the carrying off of Jehoiakim (II Chron. 36.6-7). In the Book of Daniel and in Berossus' history of Babylon from the middle of the 3rd century B.C., it is mentioned that Jewish captives were brought to Babylon by Nebuchadnezzar before his formal accession.[64] Stenring's tables show that the Captivity, reckoned in this way, lasted exactly 70 (lunar) years (events 255-297).

For the time before Josiah there are two obvious contradictions between the OT and the generally accepted account of secular history. One is the length of the reign of Pekah. The text clearly mentions 20 years and confirms this by several synchronisms. But nevertheless there must be some mistake. If—as is generally accepted, with the support of Assyrian sources—Menahem paid tribute to Tiglath-pileser III around 742[65] and Hoshea was king about 732/31, then it is impossible to insert both the rest of Menahem's reign and the reigns of Pekahiah and Pekah between these dates. Most scholars therefore agree that there is some mistake (perhaps Pekah was firstly king of only a part of Israel). In the following section, therefore, an alternative will be presented, in which Pekah is only given 4 years (as proposed by Begrich and Jepsen, among others).[66]

This alternative will also include a co-regency between Hezekiah and Manasseh. The OT very seldom tells us anything about co-regencies, even though there are many indications that they occurred. In the case of Hezekiah and Manasseh there is no possibility of constructing a co-regency within the framework of the OT itself, as after the fall of Samaria there were no kings in Israel to compare with. If, however, we accept—as the Assyrian records point out—that

---

[64] Larsson, op. cit.

[65] Thiele, op. cit., p. 98.

[66] J. Begrich, *Die Chronologie der Könige von Israel und Juda und die Quellen des Rahmens der Königsbücher* (1928). A. Jepsen, Zur Chronologie der Könige von Israel und Juda (*Zeitsch. f. Alttest. Wiss.* 1964).

Sennacherib's campaign against Lachish and Hezekiah took place around 701 B.C. and that this was the 14th year of Hezekiah's reign (II Kings 18.13), Thiele's solution of a 10-year co-regency between Hezekiah and Manasseh seems convincing.[67]

It must be emphasized that the corrected chronology thus obtained is *not* in agreement with the chronology of C but a correction of the system, which on these two points was probably wrong, compared with the real history. Table 2 shows, firstly, Stenring's deduction of the system of C, secondly, the system corrected on the two above-mentioned points and, thirdly, the probable dates of some fairly well-known events, according to Egyptian and Assyrian records.

Table 2
Comparative dates in the period of the divided kingdom until the reign of Hezekiah

Event	According to Stenring	Corrected chronology	According to Egyptian and Assyrian records
The division of the kingdom	961	935	
Expedition of Shishak	956	930	around 930
Battle of Karkar			854/53
Ahab's death	880	854	
Jehu king	866	840	
Tribute of Jehu			841
Menahem king	772	746	
Tribute of Menahem			742
Fall of Samaria	731	721	722/21
The 14th year of Hezekiah's reign	713	703	
Sennacherib's campaign			702/701

As we can see, there is good agreement between Stenring's dates corrected on the above-mentioned two points and the dates we have from Egyptian and Assyrian sources. (Of course, there can never be complete agreement between history and a schematic system constructed much later.) This agreement is remarkable. I mentioned in Chapter IV that a purely mathematical solution, based on a system of time equations, gave exactly Stenring's solution. With the above-mentioned corrections, this solution at the same time yields almost perfect agreement with the known history. This is a good

---

[67] Thiele, op. cit., p. 155.

argument in favour both of Stenring's solution and of the good historical sources of C.

In Table 3 the mathematical solution (= Stenring's) is given in terms of years of reign—as co-regent, (junior regent) and main (senior) regent—for the kings of Israel and Judah. The table shows many co-regencies. It is difficult to say whether most of them are just constructions or whether they really occurred. It *may* have been a common practice for the king to designate at a certain time one of his sons as his successor or co-ruler, in the same way as David did with Solomon.

Table 3
Years of reign in Israel and Judah according to C

	Israel			Judah	
King	Co-regent	Main regent	King	Co-regent	Main regent
Jeroboam	0	22	Rehoboam	0	17
Nadab	1	1	Abijah	14	3
Baasha	0	24	Asa	11	41
Elah	2	0	Jehoshaphat	14	25
Zimri-Tibni	4	0	Jehoram	22	8
Omri	4	8	Ahaziah	20	1
Ahab	2	22	Athaliah	0	6
Ahaziah	17	2	Joash	0	40
Jehoram	24	12	Amaziah	7	22
Jehu	0	28	Uzziah	12 y, 5 m, 5 d.	39 y, 7 m.
Jehoahaz	3	14	Jotham	0	16
Jehoash	5	11	Ahaz	8	16
Jeroboam II	11	41	Hezekiah	10	29
Zachariah	1	6 months	Manasseh	0	55
Shallum	0	1 month	Amon	0	2
Menahem	0	10	Josiah	0	31
Pekahiah	0	2	Jehoahaz	0	3 months
Pekah	0	20	Jehoiakim	0	11
Hoshea	0	9	Jehoiachin	10	3 m, 10 d.
			Zedekiah	0	11

The whole period, from the division of the kingdom to the end of the reign of Zedekiah, will thus be 374 years, 1 month and 5 days (standard calendar), according to Stenring's reconstruction of C (the real period is shorter).

THE PERIOD BEFORE THE DIVIDED KINGDOM

For the period before the divided kingdom there are few opportunities of comparison with historical sources. In Table 4 some dates are given, as calculated by Stenring and alternatively corrected in the same way as in Table 2.

Table 4
Calculated dates for some events from Exodus to David

Event	According to Stenring	Corrected chronology
Affliction begins	1641	1615
Exodus	1466	1440
Crossing of Jordan, fall of Jericho	1426	1400
End of the period of Ehud and Shamgar	1271	1245
Israel is rescued by Deborah and Barak "by the waters of Megiddo" (Jud. 5.19)	1252	1226
Saul made king	1056	1030

It was earlier supposed that the Exodus occurred around 1250. However, in the last few decades many scholars — especially archaeologists — have advocated an earlier date.[68] For example, no traces have been found of an important city flourishing in the 13th century at Jericho, and also ruins of other towns point on an earlier invasion.[69] This suits the chronology in Table 4 rather well. We also know that some time after 1600 B.C. the domination of the Hyksos in Egypt was broken by Ahmose, the founder of the Eighteenth Dynasty. Josephus was of the opinion that there was some connection between the Jewish people and the Hyksos,[70] and that the affliction began when Ahmose seized power. Of course, we do not know how much real history there is behind the tales of the affliction and the Exodus or if they are valid only for some tribes. But it is not impossible that the dates given in Table 4 are not all too wrong.

The same may be said about the date of Shamgar. In Jud. 3.31 it is mentioned that Shamgar slew the Philistines, which is the first time we hear about an actual battle between Israel and the Philistines (the rather general reference to them in 3.3 probably has not much historical value, as it is not tied to any special event). The penetration of the Philistines into Palestine is supposed to have happened around 1200 B.C. but seems to have been preceded by attacks from related peoples, as can be seen from an inscription in Karnak dated around 1220. Also in a victory inscription the Pharaoh Meneptah (probably in

---

[68] Concerning this discussion, cf. E. Drioton, La date de l'Éxode (*Rev. d'hist. et de phil. relig.*, no. 1, 1955).
[69] Cf. works of K. Kenyons especially.
[70] Josephus, *Contra Apionem*, I, 73-105.

the year 1227 B.C.) tells how he captured Askelon and Gezer (which we later know as Philistine centres) and laid Israel waste—which is the first time the name of Israel is ever mentioned, as far as we know.

In connection with the battle "by the waters of Megiddo" it may be mentioned that archaeological evidence points to the destruction of the city of Megiddo some time in the beginning or middle of the twelfth century.

Of course, not much weight can be given to the evidence of the biblical chronology for this period—a thousand years before the chronology was constructed. It is obvious from all the round periods of 40 years from the Exodus to the division of the kingdom that the real chronology was not known with any certainty. But it is interesting that there are sound reasons for thinking that the dates given are not quite impossible.

In conclusion, it may be said that for the period after the division of the kingdom there is astonishing agreement between what we know about this period from Assyrian, Babylonian and Egyptian sources and the evidence of the chronological system—purely based on biblical sources. So the chronicle material, on which C must have been based, seems to have been good. Also from the period before the division, it is very possible that the chronology gives a good idea of the main periods, but about this we know as yet too little to be sure.

Finally, it must be emphasized that Stenring does not claim that he has found the *real* chronology, only that he has found the chronological *system* used in a late reconstruction several hundred years after the events really happened. It may well be that studies of the real chronology—such as Thiele's or Jensen's—may come to other conclusions and in the same time leave Stenring's theories intact.

CHAPTER NINE

WHEN WAS THE CHRONOLOGY CREATED?

We have several times touched on the question: how old is the chronology? Questions of time are important—in archaeology, in history and in textual and source criticism. Time is also important in this connection and I shall deal with the question at some length.

Limits of the date

Let us start with what is supposed to be the last link in the chain of the twelve books which, according to Stenring, forms the first OT canon. *The Books of Chronicles* cannot, as a whole, be much older than 400 years B.C., as the last generations related in its genealogies cannot well have lived before that time. It is generally thought to be later and is often dated around 300-350 B.C. But many scholars date it still later, for example, the well-known Norwegian exegete Mowinckel.[71] In his opinion parts of the books were written after 200 B.C. Consequently this starting-point gives a date for C probably somewhere between 200 and 350 B.C.

C is part of the Hebrew version of the OT and differs in some respects from the Septuagint and the Samaritan versions. On the other hand, both these versions have so much of the chronological system that it is very hard to believe that they may be older than C. That would mean too narrow a limitation on the design of the system.

The older parts of the Septuagint version are likely to be not later than 200 B.C., which establishes a *terminus post quem*. On the other hand, is it possible that the Samaritan version was written as late as 200-350 B.C.? It is often supposed that this version should be dated to the time around the break between the Samaritans and official Judaism. According to Josephus,[72] the Samaritan Temple was built around 330 B.C. and at the same time there was a break between the Jews and the Samaritans.[73] After the new Temple had been built, there

---

[71] S. Mowinckel, *Studien zu dem Buche Ezra-Nehemia* (1965).
[72] Josephus, *Ant.*, XI, 7-8.
[73] Up to now most scholars have thought that Josephus was mistaken about the date and that the Temple was built at least 100 years earlier. The principal reason is that Josephus speaks of Sanaballet as governor in Samaria. But, according to Nehemiah and

must have been great religious rivalry between the two groups. But we have no real evidence of definite hostility before the time of the Hasmoneans in the second century. The many similarities between the Samaritan and the Septuagint versions also argue that there was not too great a difference in time between them.

Let us then go to the chronology itself. The Egyptian civil solar calendar is one of the calendars used. This argues a date when Palestine was part of Egypt, i.e. around the third century. The second calendar used—in one way the most important calendar of the system—is the standard calendar, i.e. the solar calendar with 365 days and one intercalated day each fourth year. It is a very advanced calendar. The Julian calendar was later to be based on the same principle.

The first time this calendar was introduced in history was, as far as we know, in Egypt by the Canopus Decree of 238 B.C. This Egyptian calendar innovation was obviously regarded as very important and came about through a decision by a great council of priests (as related on the Canopus Stone). In this decree the importance of the new calendar was emphasized—it would put the seasons in their right places and thus also assign the religious feasts their right places in the seasons, i.e. it was a calendar of much religious importance.

Palestine at that time was closely connected with Egypt and was ruled by the Egyptian kings. A calendar reform—introducing a year with such specific characteristics—could not have been unknown to the Jews. When we find it used in C, we must suspect some connection between the date of C and that of the calendar reform.

The probable date

This suspicion is strengthened by a remarkable fact, which Stenring discovered several years after he had worked out the system in its details. It turned out that there were exactly 3600 solar years between the beginning of the system (the Creation) and the starting-point of the new calendar at the following Egyptian New Year (22 October 238 B.C.).[74]

---

the Elephantine Papyrus, Sinuballit was governor in the last half of the 5th century. Some years ago, however, a seal of *another* Sinuballit, governor of Samaria, was found, together with several papyri, in a cave north of Jericho. This Sinuballit obviously lived around the middle of the fourth century (see a paper by Cross in *Bibl. Archaeolog.*, Dec. 1963). It may therefore well be that Josephus was right about the date.

[74] Stenring supposes that the new calendar started retro-actively, i.e. on 22 October 239 B.C. The text of the Canopus Decree, however, gives the impression that the

Both the even number and the fact that the calendar then introduced was a fundamental element in the system make the dating of C to about 230-235 B.C. probable.

Why was this particular figure of 3600 years chosen? It is, of course, an even number, which also contains the numbers 12 and 40, which are to be found in other Biblical contexts. It is also a main number in the Babylonian system of counting, which was built up on a sexagesimal division, in which the most important numbers were 60 (*soss*), 600 (*ner*) and 3600 (*sar*). These periods were also used in chronological designs in the historical writing of antiquity. Thus, the old Christian chronologist Eusebius[75] says of the Babylonian priest and historian Berossus (c. 260-280 B.C.): "In his history Berossus reckoned by *sar, ner* and *soss*." Thus, according to Berossus, 10 kings ruled over the Chaldeans before the Deluge for a period of 120 × 3600 years (Genesis also has 10 generations of patriarchs before the Deluge). From the chronological point of view, the number was of particular importance, owing to the fact that 3600 was 10 times the number of degrees in the celestial sphere.

But the choice may also have been conditioned by other reasons. In rabbinical tradition it was supposed that the Creation may have occurred (and that at any rate the reckoning of time originally began) about the vernal equinox.[76] Irrespective of whether this view also prevailed when the chronology was designed, it was natural to start from such a supposition. By this means, a close connection was obtained with the prevailing Babylonian calendar, which was possibly also used in Palestine. However, it was equally natural that, as regarded the solar calendar, the official Egyptian reckoning should be accepted, in which in 238 B.C. the first day of the year fell on 22 October (Julian calendar).

In that case the problem was to find a date when the first day of the year in the official Egyptian calendar fell approximately at the vernal equinox, for only then it would be possible to obtain a common origin for all the three calendars, an origin which at the same time fell in the right season. Three thousand five hundred solar years before the

---

calendar was to start at the following New Year, i.e. 22 October 238 B.C. With the correction given in Chap. 8, note 62, the Creation would have fallen, according to the system, in the evening of 8 April 3835 B.C., which is still exactly 3600 Egyptian solar years before the start of the new calendar.

[75] *Chronicon*, col. 8.
[76] Cf. Ettisch in *Revue de Qumran*, no. 9, p. 131.

Canopus Decree, the Egyptian New Year (1 Thoth) fell on 13 March, 3600 years before on 8 April and 3700 years before on 3 May. The next time the New Year fell in April was 1400-1500 years forwards or backwards in time. A Creation 3600 years before the Canopus Decree must have seemed suitable from all points of view.[77]

Other evidences of the time

If we suppose that the work of C was finished some time before 230 B.C., then we also get other "round" numbers. Thus, 2000 years would have passed since the Deluge. Furthermore, the following jubilee year would have been the 25th, which means that exactly 1200 years would have passed since the first one.

Stenring has an interesting hypothesis about this 25th jubilee year. Because of the very strict rules for a jubilee year, it is hard to conceive that is was ever celebrated. If it was, it is not very probable that it had been reckoned through hundreds of years. According to Stenring, the rules for jubilees were probably given at the same time as the biblical canon was established or anyhow not too long before. In that case the jubilee was meant to be celebrated. The first time when it was historically reckoned was the first jubilee after the canon had been revealed to the people. However, as the rules proved to be too radical for practical life, they were not observed. Then came the Maccabean wars and after that the year of jubilee was no longer reckoned as an independent year. Possibly it was reckoned together with the 49th year in each cycle—the seventh sabbatical year. In this form we find it in the Book of Jubilees.

One fact supporting this hypothesis is that, if we follow the years of jubilee in C and suppose that also the 25th year of jubilee was reckoned (October 205 to October 204 B.C.) but after that count only sabbatical years every seventh year, we find that these sabbatical years fall in their historically correct places. According to 1 Macc. 6.49, there was a year of rest in the 150th year (era of Sel.), i.e. in the year starting in October 163 B.C. and, according to Josephus, there was another one starting in October 135 B.C.[78] Josephus also mentions that the year starting in October 69 A.D. was a year of rest. All these facts suit perfectly a seven-year cycle, starting from October 204 B.C.

There is another fact that also fits well in the picture. It was earlier

---

[77] 3600 years also makes 72 "jubilees" of 50 years and, as we know, 72 is also used as a "round" number in the Bible and in the tradition.

[78] Josephus, *Ant.*, XIII, 234.

mentioned (p. 27) that the most probable solution of the riddle in Ex. 9.31 was that two-crop cultivation was presupposed. But, as far as we know, this system was introduced into Egypt by Ptolemy II from about 270 B.C. onward.[79]

The general chronological background, 230-235 B.C., also seems to fit well with C. We may say that this was the period of the chronologists. One generation earlier Manetho and Berossus had established their Egyptian and Babylonian chronologies or chronics, starting from the earliest times and going down to their own days. Probably the mysterious "demotic chronicle" was simultaneously being written in Egypt, giving the lengths of the reigns of several kings but in a secret, oracular way. It has been pointed out by Meyer[80] that there are many similarities in general attitude between this chronicle and the OT. Also in Egypt, in Alexandria, Eratosthenes was working on his famous chronology around 240 B.C. As has already been pointed out in Chapter III, the general background, the Hellenistic-Pythagorean thinking, the living connections between the Jews in Palestine and the Hellenistic world—especially through contacts in Alexandria—also argue in favour of the supposition that C is to be dated around 230-235 B.C. The above-mentioned "round numbers" certainly provide strong arguments in the same direction. It is, in fact, very difficult to believe that they were just the result of chance. I personally feel quite convinced that this is the right period.

[79] M. Schnebel, op. cit.
[80] E. Meyer, *Kleine Schriften II* (1910-1924).

CHAPTER TEN

MODIFICATIONS TO THE CHRONOLOGY

As is well known, there are disparities in chronology between the Hebrew, the Septuagint and the Samaritan versions of the OT. This can be illustrated by comparing three ages for the patriarchs: the age of the patriarch when he begat his first son, the remaining years of his life and the total years of his life in the respective versions.

Table 5
The ages of the patriarchs, according to the different versions of the OT

Patriarch	Hebrew			Septuagint			Samaritan		
	1st son	Remaining years	Total	1st son	Remaining years	Total	1st son	Remaining years	Total
Adam	130	800	930	230	700	930	130	800	930
Seth	105	807	912	205	707	912	105	807	912
Enos	90	815	905	190	715	905	90	815	905
Cainan	70	840	910	170	740	910	70	840	910
Mahalaleel	65	830	895	165	730	895	65	830	895
Jared	162	800	962	162	800	962	62	785	847
Enoch	65	300	365	165	200	365	65	300	365
Methuselah	187	782	969	187	782	969	67	653	720
Lamech	182	595	777	188	565	753	53	600	653
Noah	500	450	950	500	450	950	500	450	950
Shem	100	500	600	100	500	600	100	500	600
Arphachshad	35	403	438	135	430	565	135	303	438
Cain	—	—	—	130	330	460	—	—	—
Salah	30	403	433	130	330	460	130	303	433
Eber	34	430	464	134	370	504	134	270	404
Peleg	30	209	239	130	209	339	130	109	239
Reu	32	207	239	132	207	339	132	107	239
Serug	30	200	230	130	200	330	130	100	230
Nahor	29	119	148	79	79	158	79	69	148
Terah	70	135	205	70	135	205	70	75	145
Abraham	100	75	175	100	75	175	100	75	175

As will be seen from Table 5, the differences between the versions are of a very systematic character and are obviously the result of efforts to modify an original chronology with some purpose in mind. But which chronology was the original and what was the purpose?[81]

---

[81] See the discussion in La Sainte Bible, 1 : 1, pp. 171 and 230.

To start with the first question, it is not possible to prove anything with absolute certainty from Table 5. But it seems quite incredible that all the special chronological connections—also during the time of the patriarchs—which were found by Stenring could possibly have been constructed by starting with the Septuagint or Samaritan text and altering the figures in the schematic way indicated by Table 5. For this reason, we must suppose that the Hebrew chronology is the primary one.

A study of Table 5 confirms this conclusion. Let us compare, for example, the Hebrew with the Samaritan figures. The former change in a fairly irregular way, probably because they have another aim than just to show a neat and regular pattern. The Samaritan figures, on the contrary, are much more regular and on this account also more schematic. There is a certain consistency in the ages at the first sons, especially if the periods before and after Noah are looked at separately. There is a still more regular development in the total ages. Generally these ages decrease steadily from the first patriarchs to the last, with the notable exception of Noah and also of Enoch, who, according to the Scripture, did not die like the others but was taken up into heaven by God.

It is very instructive to see how the Samaritan text adapts itself to the Deluge. All the figures for the first five patriarchs and also for Enoch and Noah are exactly the same as in the Hebrew text. But the rather great ages in the latter for Jared, Methuselah and Lamech when they begat their first sons are reduced in the Samaritan text and made more similar to the ages of the other patriarchs. For this reason also the total ages of these three patriarchs must be reduced, otherwise they would not have died before the Deluge. The interesting thing is that they are reduced exactly as much as is necessary, i.e. they die in the same year as the Deluge came. So the figures in the Samaritan text may well be explained as alterations from the Hebrew text. But an alteration from the almost perfect Samaritan system to the irregular Hebrew system seems quite incredible.

Much the same can be said if we compare the Hebrew and the Septuagint systems. The Septuagint has a far more schematic and regular character. Normally the Septuagint adds 100 years to the Hebrew figures of the ages at the begetting of the first sons. But where these figures seem high enough—as in the cases of Jared, Methuselah, Lamech, Noah, Shem, Terah and Abraham—the Hebrew figures are retained (the small alteration concerning Lamech is possibly connected with some wish to place the deaths of Lamech and Methuselah in a suitable position relative to the Deluge). It is interesting that, with the exception of Lamech, the *total* years of the patriarchs are the same in the Hebrew and Septuagint versions before Shem. But after Eber the remaining years are the same, with the exception of Nahor. This change may be connected with the fact that after Shem the Hebrew and Septuagint versions do not give the total figures. Therefore the least alteration was made, if the remaining figures were retained.

Another point which confirms the primacy of the Hebrew text is the Song of Lamech (Gen. 4.24), according to which Lamech will be avenged seventy and sevenfold. This gives immediate associations with the age of Lamech in the Hebrew text (777 years). It may be mentioned that, according to Stenring's tables, Lamech—like the other patriarchs—was not only born and died on the 7th day in the 1st month of the lunar calendar but was at the same time born on another 7th day (the 7th day of the 2nd month, according to the standard calendar), which also "happens" to be the same birth-date as that of Seth, according to the solar calendar.

Through the changes made from the Hebrew text in the Septuagint and Samaritan versions, the deaths of the patriarchs fall in the same approximate order as their births. In the Hebrew version there is a seemingly hopeless disorder on this point. For example, both Shem, Salah and Eber died after Abraham. To a rational Septuagint translator, it must have seemed very hard to accept a version, according to which Shem—born 100 years before the Deluge—was still alive when the patriarch Jacob was an old man and at the same time also accept the statement that Noah did not die before Abraham was almost 60. We cannot be sure that he knew the very specific reasons why the C chronology sometimes behaves in a peculiar way. It is easy to understand the situation, if we suppose that the Hebrew version is the original and the Septuagint and Samaritan chronology represent alterations. But alterations in the other direction make no sense.

There must also have been another reason why especially the Septuagint translator could not accept the C chronology. If the translation was made in Alexandria, starting some time at the end of the third century B.C., the translator could not be unaware that, according to the official Egyptian chronology—presented by Manetho some half century before—the first "historical" Pharaohs had lived almost 3000 years before, so that there could not have been a Deluge over the whole world just 2000 years before his own time. The simplest way to avoid discussions about these things was to lengthen the time by adding another 100 years to the patriarchs' ages when they begat their first sons. An extra generation (Cain) also helped. By this process the total history was lengthened by 606 years before the Deluge and by 780 years after or in all almost 1400 years. (This also means that, according to the Septuagint chronology, the solar and standard calendars could both start in the spring, cf. p. 54. It is difficult to say whether this is significant or not.)

The Samaritan version was not quite so radical. For the period after the Deluge it followed the Septuagint concerning the ages at the birth of the first son (but excluded Cain). For the period before the Deluge, however, it retained, in the main, the figures of the Massoretic version, corrected at a few points in order to secure a more consistent chronology. In this way there was both a good connection with the Egyptians and a logical and symmetrical Scripture chronology.

In the Book of Jubilees there is yet another version. For the period before the Deluge the text follows the Samaritan chronology, but for the period after the Deluge it is not in agreement with any of the three versions. The ages at the births of the first sons are then generally about twice as great as in the Hebrew version. This avoids the most puzzling features of the chronology of C, and at the same time makes it possible for the writer of the Book of Jubilees to keep the history within the given frame — 50 jubilees or 2450 years from the Creation to the Exodus.

It is quite obvious that the redactors of all these different versions did not look upon the ages of the patriarchs as historical data but used them to develop *systems* with different purposes. C seems to have had an esoteric purpose, while the other redactors were more rational and tried to adapt the chronology to existing history (Septuagint and Samaritan version) or to some chosen period (Book of Jubilees). At the same time they tried to give it a systematic and logical appearance (a certain consistency in the ages at the births of the first sons, a general development in the total ages from the very great ages in the beginning to the more "normal" ages for the later patriarchs, a trend to let the deaths follow in the same order as the births, etc.).

The efforts to get the Jewish and the Egyptian chronologies to agree probably played an important role in the later versions. We find an echo of these efforts in Josephus and in the early Christian chronologists like Africanus and Eusebius, who all emphasized the perfect agreement between the chronology of Manetho and that of the Scripture (in its Septuagint version).

To a certain extent, such agreement could also be obtained by alterations in the chronology of Manetho. It is very interesting to see that there are clear traces of such adaptions. Thus, for example, it is obvious that the original chronology of Manetho has been systematically lengthened by introducing 20-year and 40-year additions in the reigns of certain Pharaohs. According to Helck,[82] these additions were probably the work of scholars, who used extracts from Manetho to consolidate a chronology based on Jewish sources.

However, there also seem to be examples of adjustments in the opposite direction, i.e. adjustments of the lists of Egyptian kings to the shorter era in the Hebrew text. A list of Egyptian kings which differs from Manetho's and is substantially shorter than his is to be found in the so-called *Pseudo-Eratosthenes*, a list which is said to have been taken from Apollodorus, who, in his turn, is supposed to have received it from Eratosthenes. According to Diels and Jacoby,[83] the list was probably the work of some Jewish writer, who used the names of the two famous chronographers to give authority to his work, which supported the Hebrew chronology. Thus, there seems to have been an interesting interplay, in which various forces were at work to adapt the Jewish and the Egyptian chronologies to each other.

OTHER DISPARITIES

However, the chronology of C was puzzling not only concerning the patriarchs. This being so, one would expect to find more attempts to "rationalize" it in the Septuagint and Samaritan versions. Without going too deeply into this, I will just give a few examples. One has already been given (p. 10). The seventh day in Gen. 2.2, with its hidden meaning, has in the Septuagint and the Samaritan versions been changed to the more understandable sixth day. Another example is Ex. 12.40, which fixes the sojourn of the children of Israel in Egypt at 430 years. This period is impossible from all points of view, if we interpret it in the usual way. The Bible itself effectively refutes it in a number of places (thus, for example, Moses' mother is said to be Levi's daughter).[84] Stenring gives the solution that the children of Israel

---

[82] W. Helck, *Untersuchungen zu Manetho und den Ägyptischen Königslisten* (1956).
[83] H. Diels, *Rhein. Mus.*, XXXI; F. Jacoby, *Apollodoros Chronik* (1902), p. 24.
[84] On this point the rabbinical tradition is primarily linked with the date of

means the four generations of Levi, Kohath, Amram and Aaron (cf. also Gen. 15.16), that the 430 years refer to their *combined* stay in Egypt and that the 400 years mentioned in Gen. 15.13 are their combined period of bondage. The period of time obtained from these two conditions proves to fit in between the dates fixed by other data between Jacob's arrival in Egypt and the Exodus. It is true that a design of this kind may seem peculiar. On the other hand, C in several other cases has made use of very formal solutions, in which the reader's thoughts are led into the wrong track. Anyhow this was apparently not understood by the redactors of the Septuagint and Samaritan versions, so they changed the 430 years in Egypt to 430 years "in Egypt and in the land of Canaan", which was more understandable but did not agree well with the 400 years mentioned in Gen. 15.13.

The next example of adjustments in the Septuagint seems at first sight very unimportant. According to the Hebrew text, after passing the Jordan, the children of Israel "did eat of the old corn of the land on the morrow after the passover, unleavened cakes and parched corn in the selfsame day. And the manna ceased on the morrow after they had eaten of the old corn of the land". Why did not the manna cease on the day before, the first day of the unleavened bread? The children of Israel ate corn in the morning and were anyhow not allowed to gather manna on this day, so why should the manna—God's gift—fall and lie unused? The Septuagint redactors tried to improve the text and altered it, so that it looked as if the manna ceased to fall on the very day of the unleavened bread. They did not know the reason for the statement in the Hebrew text. Manna had to cease the next day, otherwise it would not have been exactly 40 years to the day since the manna began to fall (cf. Ex. 16.35).

In his great work *The Mysterious Numbers of the Hebrew Kings* Thiele goes further into the period of the divided kingdom and makes a penetrating study of the differences between the Hebrew and the Greek manuscripts concerning the chronology. He has found

---

Abraham's vision (Gen. 15) and with the birth of Isaac, associations for which there is, however, no evidence in the text of the Bible (see *Seder 'Olam Rabbah*, Chaps. 1 and 3). According to this tradition, the children of Israel sojourned in Egypt for 210 years (according to Stenring's calculation, about 202 lunar years). As Meysing pointed out (L'énigme de la chronologie biblique, *Rev. de Qumran*, no. 22), Stenring's chronology is also close to the rabbinical tradition in other respects. See also G. Larsson: Is Biblical Chronology Systematic or not, *Rev. de Qumran*, no. 24.

convincing proofs that the Greek figures are the results of attempts to "improve" the Hebrew manuscript. I cite only the conclusion:[85]

> Putting all the facts together, the evidence seems definitively to favor the Hebrew as possessing the earliest and the most accurate figures for the kings of both Israel and Judah, and the indications are that the variants of Sept. came into being at some early period — probably in the centuries immediately preceding the beginning of the Christian era — as the result of struggles with the chronological difficulties of the Hebrew text, and that the numbers there found give evidence of efforts to produce a chronological pattern more clear and consistent than that found in the Hebrew figures. The pattern of Sept. having been brought into being, it appears that scholars of a still later period became aware of some of the inconsistencies and imperfections involved in the latter portion of that variant pattern, and in the endeavor to bring about still further improvements brought into being the variant figures now found in Lucian.
>
> It seems clear, then, that of these patterns of Hebrew chronology, that of Mass. is the earliest and best, that of Sept. comes next in point of time and accuracy, and that of Lucian is the latest and the most inaccurate.

Finally, two examples from the Book of Ezekiel may be mentioned. In Ez. 4.5 the Hebrew text tells us that one or two weeks after his great introductory vision on the fifth day of the fourth month in the fifth year the prophet lay upon his left side for 390 days, then for 40 days upon his right side. But in 8.1 it is related that in the sixth year, in the sixth month and in the fifth day he rose and sat in his house. If the same calendar was used to give the date of both the first vision and the last occasion, there would not have been time for the prophet to lie for 430 days. So the Septuagint shortens the time to 190 days and in this way also gets a more probable period for the period of the iniquity of the houses of Israel and Judah, which, according to the prophet, was as many years as the days spent lying on the left and the right sides. In the Hebrew version, however, these 430 years exactly coincide with the day when David ascended his throne in Jerusalem.[86]

In Ez. 40 : 1 the Hebrew text gives the date of the temple vision as "in the new year (the beginning of the year), in the tenth day of the month". Stenring shows that these two days are in reality taken from

---

[85] Thiele, op. cit., p. 203. An opposite opinion is argued in *Journ. of Bibl. Lit.*, 1967 : 2.

[86] About these periods of 390 and 40 years there has been much discussion (cf. Ziegler, *Ezékiel* (1954), p. 21).

different calendars, and that in this way the vision falls at the same time at the beginning of the year (which symbolizes a new period) and on the same date (the 10th day of the 5th month) when the old temple was destroyed. The Septuagint quite destroys this symbolism by rationalizing the date to "in the first month, in the tenth day of the month".[87]

---

[87] I shall give some other examples of how the Septuagint rationalized the biblical chronology. More can be found in Thiele's study. It has already been pointed out how the redactors of the Septuagint tried to get a more systematic and regular system. According to the Hebrew version, the Deluge began on the 17th day of the 2nd month and on the 27th day of the 2nd month the next year the ground was dry again and Noah left the ark. This is an uneven period, but it is fixed for very specific symmetrical reasons, as can be seen from Stenring's analyses (see p. 64 in his study). The redactors of the Septuagint altered the starting day to the 27th day of the 2nd month and thus got an exact one-year period.
In Ex. 6.20, the age of Amram is 137 years in the Hebrew version but 132 years in the Septuagint. Why? An obvious explanation seems to be that in this way the Septuagint got a descending series of ages, Isaac (180 years), Jacob (147), Levi (137), Kohath (133), Amram (132), Aaron (123) and Moses (120), which agrees well with the tendency in Table 4 for the patriarchs to be given gradually lower ages. The Hebrew version breaks this tendency but in this way makes it possible to fulfil the condition that Israel should sojourn in Egypt for 430 years and be afflicted for 400 years (see page 61). In this way the last patriarch—Amram—also died in the year 2400, a round and suitable number for the first great period in the history of Israel.
Another chronological difference in Exodus of some interest is that in Ex. 40.2 and 40.17 the Septuagint equates the first day of the month with the day of the new moon. The Hebrew version never does this for an event with a given date. The reason is that none of the three calendars used followed the actual moon. Why was this addition made in the Septuagint? Maybe there was some opposition among the Alexandrian Jews to the lunar calendar (cf. the Book of Enoch and the Book of Jubilees), and so the Septuagint stressed that the lunar calendar should be used, at any rate for religious festivals.
The slight difference in expression between the Septuagint and the Hebrew version in Lev. 25.2 is of importance. The Hebrew version can be interpreted to mean that it was formally a sabbatical year when Israel crossed the Jordan. Stenring interprets the text in this way. The Septuagint version does not afford this possibility.
The redactors of the Septuagint thought that the spies were sent out from Kadesh in the spring (Num. 13.20), as the children of Israel left Sinai on the 20th day of the 2nd month (Num. 10.11). However, an analysis of the text (cf. 11.20 and 33.16-36) shows that more than 50 days had elapsed since then and that accordingly the spies were sent out in the middle of July—the time of the first ripe grapes, as the Hebrew version rightly states. But because of the mistake in the Septuagint, a special sentence had to be added to the effect that it would be the time of the first ripe grapes *before the spies were back.* We have here an obvious example of a later "rationalization".
It is interesting to see how the Septuagint redactors tried to solve the riddle in Jos. 3.15, where the Hebrew version gives the impression that the crossing of the Jordan took place at the time of harvest. But if this means the wheat harvest—as is normally the case—the time is impossible, as the Passover was celebrated a few days later, when, of course, the wheat was not ripe. So the Septuagint text was altered to read "the Jordan overflowed all its banks, *as* in the days of wheat harvest". This is a clever solution—but

So it is interesting to note how the key chronological data are handled with much freedom and how they are often deliberately changed to suit some purpose. Also in the later pseudepigraphic writings and in the writings of Josephus we find much of the same freedom of treatment. The works of the chronological editors were still much influenced by religious and national viewpoints.

only for a translator living in Egypt and not aware of the fact that in the dry month of the wheat harvest the Jordan *did not* overflow its banks.

In I Sam. 4.18 the Hebrew text says that Eli judged Israel for 40 years. But in the Septuagint this figure is altered to 20. Obviously the Septuagint combines Jud. 13.1 (telling that after Abdon Israel was delivered into the hands of the Philistines for 40 years) and I Sam. 7.2 (telling that Israel was oppressed for 20 years after the moving of the ark, shortly after the death of Eli). Thus, the Septuagint does not reckon with the possibility that Eli and the other judges had some time in common. That this was the case is clear from Stenring's analysis.

I Sam. 13.1 puzzled the redactors of the Septuagint, who obviously thought that the events in Chaps. 13-14 followed immediately after Saul had been made king. Perhaps this was due to the similarity between 10.8 and 13.8. Anyhow in the Septuagint the redactors simply cut out 13.1 and thus removed the problem.

The Septuagint alterations in the books of Kings and Chronicles have been discussed by Thiele and are therefore left here. I will just point out that the Septuagint text tries to bridge over such direct "contradictions" as II Kings 8.26, compared with II Chron. 22.2, and II Kings 24.8, compared with II Chron. 36.9, "contradictions" which have a special significance in Stenring's analysis.

Going further to Jeremiah, we find several small but important differences between the chronologies of the two versions. Thus, according to Stenring the 70 years in Jer. 25.11 and 25.12 are *different* periods. This was not understood by the Septuagint redactor, who by a small alteration ran the two periods together into one.

The Septuagint redactor obviously found the contradiction in Jer. 52.12 (the 19th year of Nebuchadnezzar), compared with 52.29 (the 18th year), hard to resolve and therefore cut out the chronological information. For similar reasons, vv. 28 and 30 were also expunged. But this "contradiction" was important for the construction of the biblical chronology. By it, the destruction of Jerusalem was formally fixed as exactly 18 years after the accession of Nebuchadnezzar (when both the 18th and the 19th years are correct), which had further important consequences in the construction of the chronology.

CHAPTER ELEVEN

IDEOLOGICAL CONTENT AND CONNECTIONS WITH OTHER SOURCES

I have so far discussed the system, content and date of the OT chronology. A very important aspect, however, has not yet been investigated, namely, the general connection of C with the religious ideas of the time and its association with other sources of the OT. Some few remarks may, of course, be found in the earlier chapters but here I shall concentrate on these problems.

This means, however, that the study will leave the relatively safe area where hypotheses can easily be tested. Instead we shall come into an area where it is easy to set up hypotheses, but where the material for testing them is scarce or unsound. I should therefore be grateful if the reader who does not approve of what is said in this and the next chapter will not let this influence his judgement of the earlier chapters. The facts given there are not dependent on what I am going to discuss now.

Ideological background

A general method used in Bible criticism is to analyze (by literary and textual criticism or by other means) which parts of the text derive from a certain source. Then the ideas and the opinions in this source can be studied. Often the delimitation of the source and the discussion of the ideas have to go hand in hand, as the ideas may be one criterion for identifying the source.

This method is hard to use in this case and anyhow it is beyond my competence to use it. The problem is that the only things that we really know are derived from C are some of the years and dates.

In some cases, there is, however, great probability that a text has been inserted. This is true of texts like Gen. 6.3, Ex. 9.31-32, I Kings 8. 65-66 and II Chron. 7.8-10, Ez. 4.4-6, Num. 14.33-34 and at any rate parts of the story of Hezekiah's cleansing of the Temple and the celebration of the Passover (II Chron. 29 *et seq.*). But in most cases we cannot be sure that the text was not taken over from another source, perhaps after altering some dates.

So it is perhaps better to start directly with the religious ideas. Can anything be said about C's attitude? If we try to find out what is especially stressed in the chronology, we find the following points:

(1) The genealogies which at the same time provide a chronological skeleton and show Israel's right to inherit the promises given to the patriarchs.

(2) The Exodus and the following events to the crossing of the Jordan, framed by the ordaining of the Passover and Israel's passing through the Red Sea, on the one hand, and the passing over the Jordan and the celebration of the first Passover in the Promised Land, on the other hand. Within this frame lies the giving of the Law, the ordaining of Sabbaths and festivals and the scheme of God's blessing, the people's sin and God's punishment.

(3) The predominant importance that was assigned to the Passover, openly marked in the Exodus story and in the Law and especially by hidden connections like those mentioned in Chapter VI. We see from the Book of Jubilees how such date connections illustrate the writer's opinion.

(4) The general importance that was assigned to connections (often hidden) with other great sacrificial feasts.

(5) Otherwise the pillars of the chronology are the scheme of rescue and oppression (blessing and punishment) during the time of the judges, David's making Jerusalem the capital, the events concerning the Temple (its building, the finding of the Law under Josiah, Hezekiah's cleansing of the Temple, its destruction, Ezekiel's vision of the new Temple and the first celebration of the Feast of Tabernacles in Jerusalem after the Exile), the Exile and the rehabilitation of king Jehoiachin in the Exile.

(6) Efforts to raise the priestly status, for example, by letting Aaron be born on the same date as the Passover and giving him a key position in the chronological design, by stressing Hezekiah's celebration of the Passover, which is then taken as the starting-point in further securing the privileges and rights attached to the priesthood in Jerusalem, etc.

(7) The choice of Jeremiah and Ezekiel as the only prophets included in the canon and at the same time the addition of a set of important chronological data to the texts of these books.[88]

All these things make it quite clear that C in the main shared the

---

[88] It seems obvious that some parts of Jeremiah are later additions, such as Chap. 52, which in this connection is very important. Also in Ezekiel it is likely that the dates are later additions.

views of the Deuteronomists (D), the editors of the Priestly Codex (P) and the Chronicler, with their strong emphasis on the centralization of the cult worship in Jerusalem and the Temple, the importance of the sacrificial feasts and especially of the Passover and their general view of history as alternations between God's blessings and punishments, because of the sin of the people. It is also symptomatic how the fundamental data in the chronological system are to be found almost entirely in the parts which are usually assigned to these works.

Such a similarity of view naturally raises the question if there are any direct connections between the C group and the other groups of redactors. The D-P relation has been especially discussed in the exegetic literature. But now I shall study the question with C as the starting-point.

In the main there seem to be two alternatives. Either the different redactions (or tradition streams) are independent of each other, with distinct and considerable spans of time between them or they are — more or less — the result of the continuous work of a continuous group. The essential thing in the latter case is that material from different epochs of the history of Israel was not definitely fixed before in a final redactional phase, in which the opinions of the final redactors were closely expressed. Most scholars suppose that the D group and the P group worked at different times. But it is also held that there was a common redaction, which influenced the religious ideas expressed in the definitive version of the Scriptures to a considerable extent. Can the existence of C in any way solve this problem?

Connections with D and P

It is difficult to come to a definite conclusion. The chronological material used in the later history of Israel belongs almost entirely to what is supposed to be the *D* part. If this part was finished at an earlier stage than C, there must have been changes and additions when the final chronology was designed. These may, however, have been rather limited. Most of the chronological material used in C from the divided kingdom onward is probably authentic material, perhaps misused, misunderstood and supplemented but not much changed. So it may well be that the D parts of the OT are separate and older than the C parts, even though the similarity in views and the very close connection in chronology are noteworthy. It is also remarkable that the only two prophets included in the C work are Jeremiah and

Ezekiel, who are looked upon as the prophets closest to the D group.[89]

I shall, however, leave this discussion and instead concentrate on the question about C and *P*, because the conjunction between these redactions seems to me to be very striking and interesting. There are two facts which must be emphasized before we start the discussion.

(1) Almost all the chronological information in Genesis, Exodus, Leviticus and Numbers used for constructing C belongs to the parts which are traditionally assigned to P. In all these books I can only find two or three texts of chronological importance, which are usually[90] assumed to belong to other sources than P, namely, Gen. 15.13 and Gen. 7.17 (possibly also Gen. 6.3 and Num. 33.38-39). The greater parts of the story of Jacob and Laban and the death of Joseph may also come from other sources and include dates, which, however, are of less importance. Possibly these texts are late. Winnet (*Journ. of Bibl. Lit.* 1965 : 1) anyhow regards some of them as later, post-exilic insertions. This agreement between the chronology and the P source is very striking indeed.

(2) A considerable number of the dates given in these books must have been especially designed for C, otherwise C could not possibly have shown such exact agreements and be so infiltrated with symbolic meaning and mutual correspondence between dates as is the case.

With this background let us weigh the following two hypotheses against each other.

(*a*) P and C are the results of different redactions, carried out at different times.

(*b*) P and C are the results of continuous, coherent, redactional work.

If we start with hypothesis (*a*), we must then assume either that the original dates in P have been changed to a considerable extent or that the chronology never was a part of P but was added later. Are these assumptions probable?

If the original chronological information in P was *considerably* changed, it is difficult to explain why we cannot find any traces of this

---

[89] It has often been stressed that there are many obvious similarities between these two prophets, similarities which may be the results of some common redaction. Both also express to a large extent the ideas relevant to the D and P groups. Ezekiel also shows much of the same interest in the Temple and in cultic things as is characteristic of P.

[90] According to the discussion by M. Noth, S. Mowinckel and others.

in the Septuagint and the Samaritan versions. In principle these versions are obviously based on the same general chronology as the Hebrew version, only changed in a systematic way. It seems out of the question that any part of the Septuagint or the Samaritan version should contain an original version and that a systematic change of this should lead to the remarkable qualities in the Hebrew chronology. And if there had been a well-established P chronology for hundreds of years back, is it then very likely that the redactors of the Septuagint and the Samaritan version would choose the new C chronology as a basis but change it to a large extent?

On the other hand, if there never was any chronological information of importance in P, then we have to alter our view of P considerably. Chronology and genealogies are in this case very closely connected and have been looked upon as the most typical features of P. This is also because they are so closely connected with one of the main ideas of P—to show that the children of Israel were the real heirs of the old patriarchs and were entitled to receive the promises that God had given in the covenants. Of course, there is always a possibility that the genealogies in P were originally worked out without years but that the main genealogies were later supplemented with chronological information. I think, however, that most scholars would agree with me that this does not seem to be a very satisfactory solution.

So there are reasons to consider hypothesis (b) very carefully. This hypothesis does not say that *all* parts of P are essentially the work of the same group as C. Considerable parts may be earlier. It is for careful text criticism to find out to what extent there are signs of differences within what we use to call P.[91]

In his introduction to Genesis in *The Anchor Bible* E. A. Speiser writes as follows:

> It was suggested earlier that P was, in all probability, not an individual writer but an established school in continuous operation over a long period of time. In that case, the activity of such an academy would not have come to a halt after the document that we now attribute to P had assumed definitive shape. The next logical step would be precisely the kind of compilation that was ultimately the result in the present Book of Genesis, and the rest of the Pentateuch; and in that case, R (redaction) would be a late product of the P school.

---

[91] Usually different stages in the P redaction are supposed, sometimes also parallel narratives. For example, G. von Rad speaks of a P^A and P^B part. The chronological system may provide a new background and new viewpoints for a discussion of the different elements in P.

If R is substituted for C and if the redaction is supposed to include all the twelve above-mentioned books, this may be a realistic description of the course of events.

Even if hypothesis (b) is correct, considerable parts of P may be of an earlier date. Still, are there any decisive objections to supposing that the final shaping of most parts of P took place at a late date and that they are not much older than 230-235 B.C., a date which seems probable for C?

I suspect that many readers will find such a dating unlikely, as it is generally supposed that P dates from the fifth century B.C. and perhaps even earlier (but cf. Vink, see chap. I, note 1, who dates P to early fourth century). The question if there are any decisive arguments against a later dating is a case for the specialists. I shall just mention some points I have found of interest in this connection.

The redaction of P is often connected with Ezra, perhaps with the author himself, perhaps with a group around him, perhaps just with his time. But when was this time? According to the Books of Ezra and Nehemiah, Ezra lived in the middle of the fifth century B.C. But for several reasons many scholars find this incredible and place Ezra around 400 B.C. or even later.[92] No solution seems to be quite satisfactory. Ezra has, in fact, been a problem and doubts have arisen as to whether the story of Ezra can be true. Why is not a man of such importance mentioned in Ecclesiasticus, which is supposed to be based on sources from the time around 180-190 B.C., when the other prominent prophets and leaders of Israel are mentioned there? Can it be that some Ezra—perhaps fictitious, perhaps real—has been given an important role concerning the Law just to lend authenticity and antiquity to a more modern compilation?

Sometimes the proofs of the age of P are of a stylistic and linguistic character. Is it possible to decide the age of P in this way with any security? The well-known Semitist Torrey has argued very strenuously that the Book of Ezekiel was written around 230 B.C. from an older source[93] and has adduced many linguistic arguments to prove it. His opponents have tried to show that the Book was written during the Exile and they, too, have used linguistic arguments. So it seems possible that dating on a linguistic basis may yield differences of more than three hundred years.

---

[92] So S. Mowinckel in *Studien zu dem Buche Ezra-Nehemiah*.
[93] C. Torrey, *Pseudo-Ezekiel and the Original Prophecy* (1932).

Of interest in this connection is also the fact that even in the Qumran texts — probably written much later than C — there seems not to be any marked difference between the Hebrew used there and the old biblical language. As R. Meyer expresses it in an article:[94]

> Wer etwa die "Letzten Worte des Mose" (1 Q DM), eine Paraphrase zum Deuteronomium im Stile des Jubiläenbuches, die Regula communitatis (1 Q S) oder anonyme, hebräisch verfasste Prophetenworte auf ihren Stil untersucht und mit älteren biblischen Texten vergleicht, muss feststellen, dass die Schreiber von Qumran keinen Unterscheid zwischen der "klassischen" heiligen Sprache und dem von ihnen selbst geschriebenen Idiom empfinden.

Many scholars have also expressed the opinion that at any rate some parts of the Pentateuch must be fairly late. For example, P. Grelot argues (*Vet. Test.* 1955, p. 250, and 1956, p. 257) that Deuteronomy must be later — perhaps considerably later — than 400 B.C. At that time the details of the Law must have been rather fluid. According to him, the redaction of Numbers is probably older than Deuteronomy but is still later than 420 B.C. H. J. Stoebe (*Vet. Test.* 1956, p. 397) gives reason for thinking that anyhow I Sam. 17 must have been formed under the mutual influence of the Septuagint and the Hebrew version, in which case the final redaction could not have taken place much earlier than the date of the Septuagint.

Referring to the feasts mentioned in Nehemiah, Auerbach tries to show that the two most important feasts in later Judaism — New Year's Day on the first day in the seventh month and the Day of Atonement — could not possibly have been celebrated in the time of Nehemiah.[95] If this is so, the parts dealing with these things in Leviticus and Numbers must be of a later date. (It also seems to be a late construction that during Ezra's reading of the Scripture on that occasion it was suddenly realized that in the Law it was prescribed that the children of Israel should dwell in booths at the Feast of Tabernacles.)

Several other scholars have given evidence pointing in the same direction, namely, that anyhow parts of P (and perhaps D) are probably of late date. Obviously these scholars do not find definite objections

---

[94] R. Meyer, Das Problem der Dialektmischung in den Hebräischen Texten von Chirbet Qumran (*Vet. Test.*, 1957, p. 139).

[95] E. Auerbach, Neujahrs- und Versöhnungsfest in den biblischen Quellen (*Vet. Test.*, 1958, p. 337).

Connections with the Chronicler

Of interest are also the connections between the *Chronicler* and C. Their religious and political positions seem to be the same in many respects. Some important information used in the chronology comes from the Chronicler and some parts must obviously be the work of C, such as the parts relating Hezekiah's celebration of the Passover. Many scholars have placed the work of the Chronicler very late—even after 200 B.C.—so from that viewpoint he and C may very well have been contemporaries.

In connection with the Chronicler we must, however, make a distinction between those parts included in C—the Books of Chronicles (possibly excepting parts of I Chronicles) and Ez. 1-3.7—and the rest, i.e. the other parts of Ezra and Nehemiah. It has been discussed whether the same writers or group of writers were behind all these books or whether different writers and redactors were at work. Most scholars who have discussed these questions seem to agree that the latter alternative is the right one. Thus, for example, Japhet[96] demonstrates differences between the Books of Chronicles and Ezra-Nehemiah such that they cannot really have had the same origin. One such reason is that in Chronicles more modern terms and expressions seem to be deliberately excluded. "From the linguistic point of view the Book of Chronicles deviates in some important points from the tendencies and phenomena of its period, which are extant in Ezra-Nehemiah".

This fact may give rise to a hypothesis. If the Books of Chronicles were written at the same time as C to form the twelfth book in the canon or are perhaps somewhat older but were substantially changed for the same purpose, then, of course, it was in the interests of the scholars working on the canon to make the book look old to give it authority. Probably this was an important aspect, because the book to a very great extent expressed the opinions of the redactional group and had a clear religious and political aim. So they avoided all modern terms and tried to write in a slightly archaic style. Perhaps it was a similar (or even the same) group which later on also wrote the books

---

[96] S. Japhet, The supposed common authorship of Chronicles and Ezra-Nehemia investigated anew (*Vet. Test.*, 1968, p. 330).

of Ezra and Nehemiah, this time to show that the Law was essentially finished in the time of Nehemiah and to present an "official" version of how it was announced to the people after a period of forgetfulness and disobedience. Perhaps the scene described was right in the main — it was just that it happened more than two hundred years later!

To conclude, it seems probable to me that the D part of the canon was finished some time during the fifth century B.C. (as, for example, Mowinckel and Pedersen have argued)[97] but later on it was accommodated to C. There is, however, also a possibility that the work was finished in close connection with the design of C, considering how greatly dependent C is on D and vice versa. As regards P, there seems to be strong evidence that the final redactions of P and C were parts of the same continuous process, which may have taken a considerable time and in which much material from older traditions and written sources was used (also material which had already received its final form). As regards the Books of Chronicles, they are probably close in time to C and express the ideas of the C group. It is impossible for me to say if they were essentially finished before but were changed in the final redaction or if they were compiled just in order to be the final link in the canon.

---

[97] S. Mowinckel, *Det gamle Testamente*, 1, (1929). J. Pedersen, Die Auffassung vom Alten Testament (*Zeits. f. alttest. Wiss.*, 1931, p. 161).

CHAPTER TWELVE

A HYPOTHESIS ABOUT THE CANON

Up to now, this investigation has been mainly based on statements in the OT itself. There have been some comparisons with Babylonian and Egyptian records and also with other written sources, such as the Book of Jubilees. OT studies often have to be limited to this, because so little is known about the history and the conditions in Palestine during the post-exilic period (up to 250 B.C.). As it is generally supposed that the main parts of the OT canon were completed before that date, it has been difficult to find support in history for theories and hypotheses concerning the way in which this canon was established.

If, however — as I believe — some very important steps in this process have to be dated later than 250 B.C., then there are also chances that we can get information about it from history and tradition. Several hypotheses can be made against the background of the historical and traditional material. I shall here present some which seem sound to me, but they must, of course, be more thoroughly tested by the specialists in this field. Probably some of the arguments are wrong, as in most other hypotheses, but it may be worth while to present them and so stimulate thinking in this field.

SLAVERY IN EGYPT

Let us start with the narrative of the Exodus. Many scholars have found that this narrative is of a rather late date, much later than the Feast of the Unleavened Bread, perhaps also later than the adjacent Feast of the Passover. But at the same time it is obvious that this narrative was given a tremendous importance in the thinking of later Judaism and also in those parts of the OT, which are connected with the P work. It is, so to say, the central motif in this work. In the D work it is less obvious. In fact there are signs that, according to D, the most important feast was not the Passover but the Feast of Tabernacles.

Another interesting fact is that, in the form in which we find it in Ex. 1-15, this narrative shows a great knowledge of the conditions in Egypt. The descriptions of the plagues are especially exact and in fact it seems to be possible to explain all these plagues in a natural way. The narrative describes things which do not happen very often, even in Egypt, but which may happen just there. It therefore gives the impression of having been given its final form not in Palestine but in Egypt.

Was there some period in Jewish history when this narrative was felt to be a central motif by a large group of Jews, and at the same time this group or parts of it had a thorough knowledge of the conditions in Egypt? There seems to have been. According to Josephus — supported by other sources — Ptolemy Soter — later Ptolemy I of Egypt — seized Jerusalem (probably around 312 B.C.) and carried away a great many Jews as captives.[98] Josephus tells us further that his son Philadelphus (Ptolemy II) later on released not less than about 120,000 natives of Jerusalem, who were slaves in Egypt.[99] This is considerably more than the numbers given for those Jews carried away to Babylon in the Captivity. So, even if Josephus exaggerates, it seems to have been a very important group which was released.

For these Jews in Egypt the Exodus motif must have been an essential one. Probably the narrative now received its final form. Details with Egyptian local colour were added, such as the description of the plagues and the struggle between Moses and the Egyptian magicians. The narrative also gave more weight to details about the hard work the Jewish people had to do, the hostility of the Egyptians and the severity of Pharaoh and also Jahweh's punishment of them — all things that are natural for an oppressed people to describe at some length. The most important innovation was probably a closer connection between the Exodus and the Passover and the raising of the Passover to the status of principal feast of the year. As I said before, the Feast of Tabernacles had probably been the most important feast earlier — this was quite natural, as it was connected both with the New Year celebration and with the end of the growing season — two events which normally constitute the main feasts in a primitive society.

Religious revival

A people in exile has a natural need to keep together, to strengthen the ties between individuals. Obviously in those days religion was the strongest common link. So there was a revival of the keeping of the

---

[98] Josephus, *Jewish Antiq.*, XII, 7.
[99] Ibid., XII, 11.

Law, great reluctance to assimilate with the Egyptians, and especially strong feeling against mixed marriages.

When the Jews were free and returned in groups to Palestine, they carried this view with them. Many stayed in Egypt and we know that in the first half of the third century the Jewish population increased remarkably in Egypt—especially in and around Alexandria. But those who preferred to return were probably the more religious ones, like those who more than 250 years earlier had returned from the Exile in Babylon.

What did they find in Palestine? A poor land but—more important for them—a land where the commandments of the Law were badly kept, where the Temple was decayed and where even the High Priests thought more of their own power and riches than of serving God. In those days or some time later, the High Priest was Onias (II), about whom Josephus writes: "This Onias was small-minded and passionately fond of money". In Ecclesiasticus (Chap. 50) we read that the Temple was in bad shape in those days. But, more than that, there was a constant danger of and a strong tendency to assimilation with the Gentiles. It is clearly described in the Books of the Maccabees but was probably obvious long before 200 B.C. The tendencies to assimilation were expressed in things like mixed marriages, the adoption of Greek customs, etc.

The need for a moral and religious revival was obvious. In the Exile the people had had no opportunities to take part in the offerings at the Temple. What had given them strength was the rules in the Law and the history of the people. So there was a strong demand that the different sources should be collected and a sacred canon created from them, which could be an instrument for the renewal of Israel, a tool in education and a support in new afflictions to come.

The forces at work were probably to be found in the group of teachers of the Law, which had developed among the oppressed people in Egypt and which worked very much in the way described of Ezekiel in captivity: "And it come to pass ... as I sat in mine house, and the elders of Judah sat before me" (Ez. 8.1). Like Ezekiel, they were probably priests or levites and, more seldom, ordinary men. They largely shared the views of the Jerusalem priests about the centralization of the cult in the Temple and the importance of the work of the priests and levites but would give more importance to the levites than the higher priests had been willing to accept before.

This background to the canon is, as I have said, a hypothesis and what has been stated in the earlier chapters and what is going to be stated later in this chapter do not depend on whether this hypothesis is true or not. But it seems to me that there is great probability in it. For example, it is obvious that Egypt plays a great role in the first canon. I have mentioned the detailed knowledge of Egypt shown in the Exodus narrative. Other examples can be found in many places in the Scripture, in the stories of the patriarchs, in the regulations in the Law, even in the exact formulations of many of these regulations.[100] There are also striking similarities between the OT and many Egyptian expressions and habits.[101] It is also striking how even a prophet like Ezekiel, who is said to have worked in Babylon, has practically nothing to say about that country and its punishment for having destroyed Jerusalem and the Temple. Instead several prophecies deal with the destruction which is to fall on Pharaoh and his people. Ezekiel sounds much more like a man of a people subdued by Egypt than by Babylon. Torrey has given reasons for thinking that the final redaction of the Book of Ezekiel took place around 230 B.C.[102] Most scholars disussing it have argued against this date. As far as I can see, there is no quite conclusive evidence that Torrey is wrong on the whole, even if some of his arguments are.

In this connection there is a small detail of interest. According to Neh. 8, when Ezra read the Law to the people, it was discovered that it was written in the Law that the children of Israel should dwell in booths at the feast of the seventh month. It would be very remarkable if such a thing suddenly became known. Mowinckel explains the notice as a new custom brought by the Jews from Babylon.[103] He also finds support in the ordinance in Lev. 23.40 that the people were to use for building booths "willows of the brook", which are found in Babylon but seldom in abundance in the dry region of Judaea. However, willows are also found in the delta land in Egypt around Alexandria. What is more, a feast of booths was also celebrated[104] in Egypt, as was not the case in Babylon.

So it is easy to find influences from Egypt. Probably it is also possible to find influences from the Greek and the Hellenistic world. Torrey, for example, finds that the theophany which is described at

---

[100] J. Rabinowitz, *Jewish Law* (1956).
[101] A. S. Yahuda, *The Language of the Pentateuch in Its Relation to Egyptian* (1933).
[102] C. C. Torrey, *Pseudo-Ezekiel and the Original Prophecy*.
[103] S. Mowinckel, *Studien zu dem Buche Ezra-Nehemia*, III, p. 172.
[104] Kristensen, *De loofhut en het loofhuttenfeest in den egyptischen cultus*.

Ezekiel's first vision is of the sort which we should expect to find in the Book of Enoch. Nothing in the description makes a Babylonian origin plausible. "The one close analogy is to be found in certain coins and low reliefs of the Ptolemaic period, in which winged creatures of composite form rest on a structure in which *wheels* are a conspicuous feature"[105] Several scholars have stressed that the narrative in Num. 16 shows the definite influence of Greek cosmology. Like the ten Atlantides (see Plato's dialogue *Critias*), ten children of Jacob were born in 4 years, according to Stenring's findings. There are similarities between the law of purity and the Pythagorean rules. As has already been mentioned, much of the number mystique found in the chronology shows the same influence. Perhaps the magic significance of the number 40 is a loan from the same sources. But the Greek-Hellenistic influence in the OT is definitely less than in later Jewish writing. The men working on the canon were probably against assimilation with the Gentiles.

BACKGROUND, IDEAS AND CREATION OF THE CANON

On the other hand, it was necessary to co-operate with the old religious leaders—the higher priests of the Temple. To create a sacred canon without their support would have been impossible at that time. In fact all those involved had most of their interests in common. Both groups wanted a strong centralization to Jerusalem—anyhow for the sacrifices. The Samaritan were fighting for their temple on Mount Gerizim and to vindicate the Temple at Jerusalem was a necessity.[106] Therefore it must have suited all the parties well to give great importance to the Passover celebration and the Exodus story and to make the Temple and the sacrifices there play a central role in the feast. In the same way great stress was laid in the P work, in Ezekiel and in the Chronicles on details of rites, priestly vestments, the dimensions and equipment of the Temple and, of course, the sacrifices. To include these things in the canon would give them

[105] Torrey, op. cit., p. 99. However, many scholars have later put forward arguments for a Babylonian origin.

[106] It is generally supposed that one of the main motives of the Chronicler was to support the superiority of the Temple in Jerusalem and the Judaean form of Judaism. It is very natural to suppose that this was also a very important reason for creating a canon—arranged from the Judaean point of view—at this particular time. After the building of the temple on Mount Gerizim, the Samaritan claims must have been felt as a deadly threat. So Rudolph argues that Chronicles was mainly written to refute the Samaritans.

importance and preserve them for the future. The genealogies and the emphasis on the sons of Aaron and on the Zadokites strengthened the position of the higher priests, and the emphasis on the levites—especially in the Chronicles—strengthened *their* position.

The religious ideas expressed in the canon were certainly supported by all the priests. Obedience to and worship of Jahweh was to be the principal thing in the life of the people. The relation between their fathers and Jahweh had been established by several convenants and the people were the lawful heirs to the promises given. If they followed the commandments and rules, everything would be in order and they would live undisturbed in their country. But if they were sinful and disobedient, the wrath of Jahweh would fall on them.

As regarded the political leadership, there was more room for differences of opinion. Those who returned home probably had no great opinion of the leadership of the High Priests. They were dreaming of a future as in the time of David. Such ideas are especially clear in the Books of Chronicles but can also be found in other places in the OT, for instance, in II Sam. 7.16. In the chronology one of the key points is the rehabilitation of Jehoiachin in the Captivity. To those longing for a Davidic kingdom, this must have been an important event.[107] Ezekiel looks forward to the days when a prince will lead the people, together with the priests.

It may well have been that there was some idea that the history of Israel would repeat itself. The parallel between the Captivity and the homecoming from Egypt in the third century and the affliction and the Exodus more than a thousand years earlier was obvious. Perhaps history would follow the same course? After their oppression by other people and their fight for deliverance, the people would once more be free and a king of the tribe of David would lead them. Ezekiel dreams of a new division of the country between the tribes (and attaches special importance to the area which is to fall to the Temple, the priests and the levites) and of the building of a new Temple like that of Solomon.

---

[107] In his work *The Pharisees* L. Finkelstein comments on this event as follows: "The historian of the period attached such importance to the event that he considered it a suitable climax to his history of Israel. King Jehoiachin himself, doubtless moved with unutterable joy in his innermost heart, named the son who was borne to him after his release, *Pedaiah*, 'YHWH hath redeemed'. And, indeed, it must have seemed to many observers that it was not only the King, but his people, who had been restored to divine favor. The hope of a restoration suddenly took on new life and strength; the impossible was fast becoming the probable".

Probably the High Priests were not fond of kingdom ideas, and the views on the political organization are a little vague and contradictory in the OT. But, as the canon was established during a time when Israel was governed by other people, the thought of freedom and future political power could anyhow not be expressed too clearly.[108] So also on these points it was possible to agree, even though opinions were a bit divided.

The material used was traditions and written sources which to a large extent were taken over as they were, with no great changes, but supplemented with new writings.[109] In Chapter XI I have already discussed the combination of the material. Besides the historical parts, the redactors wanted to include prophetical material, which would express their ideas more clearly. The Books of Jeremiah and Ezekiel were completed. They are in many respects similar to each other and have an ideological basis which in the main coincides with the other books included in the canon. These two books were originally the only ones of a straight prophetical character. Isaiah, Daniel and the twelve prophets were not yet completed as books but were compiled later. They also sometimes express views which are not as close to those of the redactors of the canon as those of Jeremiah and Ezekiel.[110] To

---

[108] Maybe this is the reason why the Book of Ezekiel—written in a time of foreign dominance—cannot speak of a king governing an independent people, but only of a "prince" as head of the people.

[109] Actually, we seem to have very little definite information concerning the written sources of the OT during the period just after the Exile. Engnell and others have supported the view that most of the tradition was oral until a late stage. Even texts supposed to belong to the J source, and consequently looked upon as old, have been questioned. For example, F. Winnet in a paper entitled "Re-examining the foundations" (*Journ. of Bibl. Lit.*, 1965 : 1) finds strong reasons for believing that large and essential parts of the J version are post-exilic work and close in time to the P work.

It seems to me that it may be quite possible that the redactors of the final canon had only a few written sources or sources written down only a few hundred years ago, besides the old chronicles from the divided kingdom. Instead their work was mostly founded on oral traditions, including the Law. It may well be that all this material was kept as a property and partly as a secret by the priests, as we know to have been the case in many other religions. It is significant that in the books of the prophets few allusions are made to specific events in the history of Israel or to specific ordinances. Would that have been the case if these were well-known matters at this time? (Compare the many direct references of this kind in the NT.) It may also be important that Jeremiah (Jer. 18.18) opposes the claim of the priests that the Torah was their special prerogative (cf. the article by Ph. Hyatt in the *Journ. of Bibl. Lit.*, 1941), which would hardly have been made if the Law was common knowledge.

[110] It has been stressed how similar the books of Jeremiah and Ezekiel are in many respects and how well they agree with the views of official Judaism and thereby also with the views of the other ten books of the first canon. Of the other great prophets,

these two was also added some chronological information of great significance.

In this way the canon Samuels, collected. It was made up of the twelve books of Genesis, Exodus, Leviticus, Numbers, Deuteronomy, Joshua, Judges, Samuels, Kings, Jeremiah, Ezekiel and Chronicles (including Ezra 1-3.7, but perhaps not I Chronicles or parts of it, as no new information for the chronological system can be found in this book). It is possible that Chronicles was entirely re-written and the other books were amplified, but, as yet, it is difficult to say to what extent. It was probably thought to be important to limit the canon to exactly twelve books—like the number of the tribes of Israel and the number of the "heads of mankind" from Adam to Jacob.

It was also important to bind the canon together by the strongest possible tie—a common chronology. How essential this was can be seen from the very refined way in which it was constructed, the extremely close co-ordination between the text and the dates, and the special meaning behind many of the dates and the periods of time. It is, in a way, understandable that this remarkable system, full of significance, was not given to the public but kept for the initiated—like the secrets of the Pythagorean brotherhoods, which to a large extent were probably also of a numerical character.

Perhaps also the designers of the system thought of the canon as something dangerous for the ordinary man. There is a common idea in many ancient religions that too much knowledge of holy things may be dangerous to men. We find this thought also in the narrative of the Tree of Knowledge and the first sin. I Sam. 6 : 19 relates how the Philistines were smitten by a serious disease when they brought the ark of God into their cities and also how even many Israelites were killed because they had looked into the ark. Only sanctified men could deal with holy things without danger.

Was it not then dangerous to reveal the canon in full to the people? There is a story in the Talmud about a lad who was reading the first chapter of the Book of Ezekiel in so absorbed a fashion that a flame came out from the text and consumed him. So it may have been

---

Proto-Isaiah is more concentrated on social evils, sometimes rejets violently the Temple sacrifices (as in Is. 1.11-15) and seems in many ways to present other views than those of the higher priests at Jerusalem. Deutero-Isaiah's vision of Jahweh as the God of all peoples is too universalistic to agree well with the ideas of the P work. According to S. Zeitlin (*The Rise and Fall of the Judaean State*), the Sadducees looked upon God as an ethnic God, the God only of the children of Abraham, Isaac and Jacob. The Pharisees, on the other hand, regarded God as the God of the whole human race.

considered prudent to take some precautions and conceal some of the holy things. If the people heard the written words and yet did not understand all the secret meaning, the risk was obviously less. It was still less so if God's holy name was also excluded from the reading. The name was never mentioned in public and it had even to be written by special scribes and in a special way. The mere handling of the holy books "defiled the hands".[111]

All over the ancient world we find traditions that holy things could not be revealed to other than certain initiated and purified persons. Esoteric knowledge is met with in most religions and also in their written sources.

A new alphabet?

Thus, the canon came to contain a secret chronological system. But it also seems to have been written in secret or anyhow archaizing characters. We have, in fact, no writings in Square Hebrew script dating from before the second century B.C. It is often supposed that the change from the older alphabet to the new script proceeded gradually after the Exile. From different parts of Syria and Egypt we have fragments written in similar but more "italic" characters. But we know from both Maccabean coins and from the Qumran writings that the old script was used as late as the last few centuries before Christ—probably side by side with the new Hebrew one. The Samaritan Pentateuch is also written in the old way.

If we compare the Aramaic "italic" alphabet found in Syria and Egypt with the very regular and specific Hebrew characters, it seems to me very difficult to think that the later developed from the former in a "natural" way. In that case one would have expected a gradually more simplified writing. But here the change is in the opposite direction. The Hebrew characters are much more "formal" and more archaic, in fact, quite strange against the background of the older characters.

So Stenring has ventured the hypothesis that the new Hebrew alphabet was formed just for the purposes of the canon. There is much evidence to support such a hypothesis—especially against the Egyptian background. At this time the simplified demotic characters were normally used there. But for writing of a "holy" and purely

---

[111] S. Zeitlin, A historical study of the canonization of the Hebrew Scriptures, *Proc. of the Am. Acad. for Jew. Res.* (1931-32).

religious content, the hieratic alphabet was used—an older, more rigid form of script between hieroglyphs and demotic writing. For people used to Egyptian conditions, it was therefore natural that sacred texts—especially old ones—should be written in special, more rigid characters of a more old-fashioned type. It also gave an impression that the text itself was old, an impression which the redactors of the canon wanted to give. In this connection it is interesting to note that in the tradition Ezra both wrote down the Torah and invented the new alphabet. At the same time the text was more difficult to read for the common people, which was probably also a desired effect.

A development from the "italic" to the new Hebrew characters is thus hard to understand if it is not supposed that the latter were formed in a consciously archaic style in some religious connection. What connection would be more natural than the establishment of the first canon? As far as I can see, the date of the new Hebrew alphabet fits the date of the canon perfectly. The general idea of the alphabet also agrees very well with the hidden chronology, the differences in an archaic direction in the Books of Chronicles, compared with Ezra and Nehemiah, etc.

The Great Synagogue and Simon the Just

In what way was the canon presented to the people? We can only guess. Perhaps the scene given in Neh. 8, in which Ezra the priest reads the Law to the people, gives a fairly good description. Perhaps Ezra is just a symbol, which could later on be used to give some sort of authorization of age to the canon. (cf. p. 76).

But information about the way of actual presentation is less important than information about the circles in which the canon was prepared. In this connection I think the tradition of the Great Synagogue or the Great Assembly is highly interesting. Many scholars have doubted the existence of this institution. Zeitlin says:[112] "Had they made a thorough investigation of the Tannaitic literature, they would not have come to such a hasty conclusion. The institution of the Great Synagogue was not a myth and the rabbis did not invent it. It was a reality and it had great influence in helping to shape the history of the Jews during the Second Commonwealth". Finkelstein[113] stresses its importance: "Such importance attached to the decisions of

---

[112] S. Zeitlin, ibid.
[113] L. Finkelstein, op. cit., p. 576.

this Assembly that it became known in later Jewish history as 'The Great Assembly' (*Keneset Ha-Gedolah*), par excellence".

When did this assembly meet? In the Mishnah treatise entitled *Abot* it is stated that Simon the Just was one of the survivors of the Great Assembly. Simon the Just was the son of the High Priest Onias II and was himself High Priest from around 220 to 180 B.C. In that case we have to assume that the assembly finished before 220 B.C., otherwise Simon would probably have been "head" of the assembly. Anyhow it would not have been anything extraordinary that he survived for 35-40 years after the assembly. It thus seems very possible that the assembly finished around 230 B.C. or a few years later. Even if Simon was then rather young, it is very natural that he should have been a member, as a son of the High Priest.

According to another Talmudic tradition (*Baba Bathra* 14 *b* and 15 *a*) "the men of the Great Synagogue wrote Ezekiel, the Twelve Prophets, Daniel and Esther". This statement must be wrong, at any rate as regards Daniel and probably Esther. As for Ezekiel, there is much evidence of a redaction, perhaps of a very profound nature, around 230-240 B.C. As far as we know, the Book of the Twelve Prophets was finished some time later. The important thing, however, is not whether the tradition is right or wrong concerning all the writings but that we have a strong tradition that a very important assembly was working on biblical books at a time which seems to be close to the date of the first biblical canon—fixed with great probability by the chronology. This does not mean that the assembly, as such, was a working body. It may very well be that the canon was the result of work done for decades by one or more groups but that the assembly had to confirm the results.

In this connection Simon the Just may have played an important role. At the time of the final work on the canon and the chronology, he may have been around 30 years of age or somewhat less. We know from the description in Ecclesiasticus (Chap. 50) that 40-50 years later he was still a magnificent man, performing the functions of High Priest with much dignity. He had caused the Temple to be rebuilt after a long period of decay. Perhaps the description in Ez. 40 *et seq.* can be seen as a plan—at any rate a wish—for the work to be done, drawn up in the circle of the Temple priests. If there was a group working on the canon around 230 B.C., it is very probable that, as the son of the High Priest and as a young, energetic and intelligent man, he took an active part in this work. We do not know if this is also true, as regards the chronology. Anyhow it is very improbable that as a High Priest some years later he would not have had any knowledge of it. This is maybe the reason why a single jubilee year really was reckoned at the end of the third century B.C.—as Stenring argues. To reckon such a year, it was necessary to know the starting-point for the jubilees and also the total span of time, i.e. the total chronology. But as the rules for a jubilee year were difficult to follow, the jubilee year was amalgamated with a sabbatical year, the period was changed from 50 to 49 years and the year became a mere theoretical construction.[114] The secret of the chronology was possibly lost some time after Simon, when his son Onias III was driven away as High Priest, Jason and Menelaus took over, Antiochus IV defiled and dilapidated the Temple, tried to destroy Judaism and caused the long and bitter Maccabean wars.

INTRODUCTION OF A NEW CALENDAR?

Perhaps this Great Assembly—or something like it—also decided other things. In the P work it is stressed that the spring month of Abib is to be the first month of the year. There is a striking similarity between the old New Year feast in the autumn with the Feast of Tabernacles and the later New Year feast in the spring and the Feast of the Passover. This parallelism is also found in the chronology (note the evidences that the Exodus in fact happened in the autumn, see p. 26-28). It is well worth asking whether the change from the view in the D work, where the autumn feast seems to be the most important, to the view in the P work, where the cultic legend of the Exodus and the Feast of the Passover are in the focus of interest, have some connection with a calendar reform. The change to spring reckoning is normally supposed to have taken place earlier than in the middle of the third century.[115] But do we really know? Even if the Babylonian

[114] So in the Book of Jubilees.
[115] For example, Thiele, Finegan and others suppose that the change in the calendar happened around 605 B.C., when Palestine came under the domination of Babylon. They base their argument especially on texts like Jer. 36.22. The general belief that the Jews in Palestine used the Babylonian calendar in the period after the Exile is mainly founded on the use of Babylonian names for the months in some books of the OT, as well as on the explicit mention of the month of the Passover as the first month (Lev. 25.5). But if this latter text was inserted when the chronology was established and at the same time all the other texts of interest in this connection are of later origin, we have in fact no real proof that any Babylonian calendar was used in Palestine in the period soon after the Exile. The first work in which only the Babylonian names are employed is probably *Megillat Ta'anit*, the "Scroll of Fasting" (maybe from the beginning of the

calendar was sometimes used in some of the later books of the OT, can we really take it for granted that this was the calendar in normal use when the events described happened? The chronology and the calendar in question are bound so closely together in the Bible that one may well suspect that one of the aims of the chronological system was to emphasize a change in the calendar.

Perhaps it was a question of introducing the lunar-solar year of later Judaism. In the Book of Jubilees, there is strong opposition to this:

> For there will be those who will assuredly make observations of the new moon—how (it) disturbs the seasons and comes in from year to year ten days too soon. For this reason the years will come upon them when they will disturb (the order) and make an abominable (day) the day of testimony, and an unclean day a feast day, and they will confound all the days, the holy with the unclean, and the unclean day with the holy; for they will go wrong as to the months and Sabbaths and feasts and jubilees.

The Book of Jubilees is supposed to have been written in the second century, like those parts of the Book of Enoch which plead for the same calendar as the former book. If this lunar-solar calendar was introduced several hundreds of years ago, it is not likely to have met with such strong opposition at this late date. But if the calendar was introduced in 230-235 B.C., the opposition is quite reasonable.[116]

---

first century A.D.; see Finegan, op. cit., p. 39). A. Jaubert (*La date de la Cêne*, Paris 1957) argues that the previous sun calendar was not changed before 170 B.C. by the pharisees against a hellenistic moon calendar.

[116] It is also possible that this was the time when the religious calendar—starting in spring—was introduced. Probably the secular and the religious calendars were used in parallel, as in Egypt and Babylon. The Talmud speaks of two principal new years, one in the autumn and one in the spring. In the OT itself, Ex. 23.16 places the end of the year in the autumn. But in Lev. 23.5 the month of the Passover, the spring month, is said to be the first of the year. Hanhart (cf. note 23, Chap. III) has found that two calendars are used in the Books of the Maccabees. Secular events are given in a calendar starting in the autumn, events with religious importance in a calendar starting in the spring.

It is very possible that the stress laid on the Passover is one of the means used to introduce this new calendar. It has often been supposed that the Passover was an old spring festival, which at a rather late date was connected with the Exodus story and fixed on a definite date. Perhaps this was done in the creation of the canon? Morgenstern (*Vet. Test.* 1955, p. 34) even asks whether the stressing of the 14th as the day of the Passover celebration is not evidence of a dispute between the Judaean and the Galilean parts of the country, with their different seasons for starting the spring harvest. But the Feast of Tabernacles also started on the evening between the 14th and 15th days, exactly six months after the Passover. So fixing the Passover celebration on the evening of the 14th day may also have been deliberate parallelism, to emphasize that in the new calendar the Passover would have the same position as the Feast of Tabernacles in the old.

An interesting hypothesis is put forward by Strobel,[117] who maintains that in principle the Essene calendar—the calendar of the Book of Jubilees—has its starting-point in 234 B.C. This was the first year in which the Tanitic year (the "standard" year), introduced by the Canopus Decree, was brought into use. As this type of year plays so important a role in the OT chronology, it is very possible that an opposing calendar—like the Essene one—would start at the same time.

The lunar and the standard year constitute at the later time the foundation of the OT chronology and that of the lunar-solar reckoning, on which the official Jewish calendar was based (the standard calendar must have been a very valuable aid to the priests of the Temple in settling intercalated months and other irregularities in the lunar year). At the same time the use of the Egyptian solar calendar provides strong evidence that the chronology was designed when Palestine was part of Egypt and when it was therefore necessary to consider the official Egyptian civil calendar.

To summarize, there are possibilities that the introduction of the biblical canon, with its new chronology, was also combined with changes in the alphabet and the calendar, perhaps also in feasts connected with the calendar. The canon, alphabet and calendar were three pillars of Jewish life and culture. Can it be that also a fourth pillar—the synagogue—was established in the same time?

Connection between the Canon and the Synagogues

In fact, there are no traces of synagogues before the date of a tablet telling of the erection of a synagogue in Alexandria in the time of Ptolemy III Euergetes (died 221 B.C.). Scholars have very often supposed that the institution of the synagogue had its roots in the Exile and have pointed to the Book of Ezekiel, according to which his prophecies seem often to have been revealed in the circle of some assembly, "and the elders of Judah sat before me" (Ez. 8.1). It is easy to think that these were meetings for preparation for the Sabbath or for worship during the Sabbath. As this is an interesting idea, I have made a check on the weekdays, according to Stenring's tables. It turned out that, of all the given dates for Ezekiel's visions and prophecies (13), *all but two* fell on the day before the Sabbath or on

[117] *Rev. de Qumran*, no. 11.

the Sabbath or on New Year's Day. These two events (event 269 and 272) were fixed by other considerations. The prophecy about the fall of Jerusalem (269) had to fall on the same date as the real fall and Nebuchadnezzar's coming against Jerusalem (272) had, according to II Kings 25.1, to happen on the tenth day in the tenth month. This close connection with the Sabbath can hardly be due to chance. So also C seems to suppose that Ezekiel's prophecies were made at "synagogues".

Even if such meetings were natural in the Exile, there was a different situation after the return to Judaea, when the remnant of the people gathered round the rebuilt Temple and the cult was centralized there. In fact, a scene like that described in Neh. 8 is hard to understand if the Law had been studied publicly in synagogues before that time and, as I said before, this scene may have had more similarity with what happened in the third rather than in the fifth century. It is quite possible that the idea of gathering to study the Law was not revived before the next Exile—the exile in Egypt during the first half of the third century.

Anyhow we may conclude that we have as yet no real evidence of any synagogue institution before the canon was created around 230-235 B.C. It is also remarkable that this institution is never mentioned in the late books of the OT and not even in Ecclesiasticus. If the Law was not finished before that time, is it very likely that it was openly read? Is it, in fact, possible that there was such a regular institution as the synagogue without the canon?

The new activity

At any rate it is quite obvious that there was a tremendous increase in the spiritual life of the Jewish people after the last half of the third century. Between the Exile and that time, very little is known about the secular and religious history of Palestine. We do not know for sure how much of the OT was written during that period. Otherwise there are few signs of any activity outside the priestly circles. After 200 B.C. we find an increasing and abundant stream of religious literature and of active groups of pious people who, like the Hasideans, the Pharisees and the like, gradually converted the religious thinking of the whole people. We find an intensive study of the Law and the Prophets by schools of scribes and the development of a very important oral Law supplementing the Scriptures. Before 200 B.C. the religious and political power seems to have rested almost completely in the hands of the Temple priests and the tribal chieftains. But later the power was partly taken over by the Sanhedrin, consisting of both priests and plebeian scribes (cf. Finkelstein, op. cit.).

Where is the source of all this activity to be found? If the Law and the system of religious institutions was in the main finished in the fifth century—as many scholars think they were—why did this activity start just 200-300 years later? Why did Jewish history and the development of Judaism still rest in almost complete darkness during all this time? With a canon completed around 230-235 B.C. and all the possible innovations connected with it, such as calendars, feasts, alphabet, synagogue institution, etc., the sudden explosion in the cultural and religious life of the Jews is much more understandable.

Part of this development is shown in the later completion of the Prophets and the Scriptures. Probably the higher priests did not like this expansion of the canon. They wanted the canon as it was, they wanted the period of prophecy to be finished. The old canon supported official Judaism, the cult, the Temple service, the sacrifices and the judicial power of the priests, according to the Law. Prophecy, on the contrary, has an element of revolution. But the High Priests could not stop the collection of new books by the scribes and the pious. Rightly or wrongly, these books were connected with prophets and great men in Jewish history. When the power and the prestige of the higher priests decreased after the death of Simon the Just, when evil men seized the office of the High Priest itself and when the secret of the original canon was more or less lost, the canon was extended with some of these new books. At first the prophets were finished and later on the Scriptures. The process did not end before the first century A.D. For some time Chronicles seems to have been excluded from the canon, partly because most of its content had already been related in the other historical books and probably also because the book gave too great an importance to the sons of Aaron, the Levites, the Davidic lineage and the old families. This did not suit either the Hasmoneans or the new class of religious leaders very well. Later on the book was included in the canon but as part of the later collection—the Scriptures. The production of new books continued in the centuries around the birth of Christ. Most of them were never included in the OT but became the Apocrypha and the pseudepigraphic writings.

From these opposed forces, grouped around the higher priests and the plebeian scribes respectively, the two parties of the Sadducees and the Pharisees gradually emerged.

The canon and the reforms connected with it started a mighty development. There were also elements of disintegration in it. The Samaritans — composed of Israelites and Gentiles — were suspicious of the centralization of the cult in Jerusalem and feared the dominance of the southern Jews. They tried to keep their own religious traditions, concentrated around Mount Gerizim. At some time — Josephus says that it was in the time of Alexander the Great — they built there a temple of their own. Anyhow, from this time a strong rivalry developed between the Samaritans and the Jews. One of the main reasons for establishing the first canon must surely have been to support the preference of Jerusalem, its Temple and its priesthood. After the establishment of the canon, the struggle must have been bitter. Many of the additions made in that connection were unacceptable to the Samaritans. So they denied all the books but the Pentateuch, which was accepted after some modifications. At that time the translation into Greek (the Septuagint) had started in Alexandria. The Samaritans had a strong colony there and so we find many similarities between the Septuagint and the Samaritan Pentateuch.

These things are partly hypothesis. It is difficult to prove how things really happened. But in my opinion there are strong reasons for thinking that the 70 years from 250 B.C. may have been of the same or greater religious importance to Judaism as the 70 years of the Captivity. From the intense work of a group in Jerusalem some time around the middle of the third century — probably with close contacts with Egypt and the Jews in Alexandria — something very important was created. For the pious in Israel this was a tremendous stimulus, a base and a weapon in their fight against assimilation with the Gentiles. At this base the Jewish thinking and belief was formed and a spiritual armour was hammered out. It gave the people strength. It roused the anger of Mattatias, when he smote with his sword the Jewish man sacrificing to the foreign gods. From this event onwards, light fell anew on the Jewish people and it saw its way through history, bearing the burden and enjoying the happiness of a people chosen by God. We still have only a feeble idea of the process which formed the Jewish belief, but we cannot fail to recognize the strength it gave, a strength of which no people in the world had more need during the evil centuries to come.

APPENDIX I

THE CALCULATION OF CERTAIN DATES IN THE CHRONOLOGY

The following account is intended to illustrate with a few examples how certain of the more important dates in the chronology of the Bible were calculated and at the same time to show how this calculation provides a check on the system as such.

The first example refers to the time of the Flood. Gen. 5.32, states that, when Noah was 500 years old, he begot Shem, and Gen. 11.10, that, when Shem was 100 years old, he begot Arphaxad, two years *after* the Flood. Since the Flood occurred in the year in which Noah became 600 years of age (Gen. 7.11), there seems to be a contradiction here. One hypothesis is that this contradiction is due to the reckoning of Noah's age in lunar years and of Shem's in solar or standard years.

Since, as far as Noah, the genealogical table gives clear time intervals, provided that we assume that each year is to be reckoned as an exact year, with no surplus or deficit of days, we obtain the result that Noah became 500 years of age 1556 years and 6 days (more exactly, on the borderline between the 6th and the 7th days) after the beginning of Creation and consequently became 600 years of age on the 7th day of the 1st month of the year 1657. The context shows that these are lunar years of 354 days. According to Gen. 7.11, the Flood began on the 17th day of the 2nd month of this year and lasted for just over a year. According to Gen. 8.14, the earth was completely dry on the 27th day of the 2nd month (of the year 1658, that is) and thus the Flood was over at that time.

The information about the 27th day of the 2nd month may have been derived from the lunar, solar or standard calendars, which gives us three alternatives. Arphaxad was born two years later, and these years may be lunar, solar or standard years. Thus we have altogether nine alternatives for the date of Arphaxad's birth:

(1) 27/2 in the lunar calendar + 2 lunar years =
    27/2 in the year 1660 in the lunar calendar
(2) 27/2 in the lunar calendar + 2 solar years =
    20/3 in the year 1660 in the lunar calendar
(3) 27/2 in the lunar calendar + 2 standard years =
    21/3 in the year 1660 in the lunar calendar

92   APPENDIX I

(4) 27/2 in the solar calendar + 2 lunar years =
    5/2 in the year 1610 in the solar calendar
(5) 27/2 in the solar calendar + 2 solar years =
    27/2 in the year 1610 in the solar calendar
(6) 27/2 in the solar calendar + 2 standard years =
    28/2 in the year 1610 in the solar calendar
(7) 27/2 in the standard calendar + 2 lunar years =
    4/2 in the year 1609 in the standard calendar
(8) 27/2 in the standard calendar + 2 solar years =
    26/2 in the year 1609 in the standard calendar
(9) 27/2 in the standard calendar + 2 standard years =
    27/2 in the year 1609 in the standard calendar

The year 1660 in the lunar calendar is, on the whole, equivalent to the years 1610 in the solar calendar and 1609 in the standard calendar.

These dates may now be compared with the information that Shem was 100 years old two years after the Flood. In this connection there are two possibilities—it is a question of either 100 solar years (= 36,500 days) or 100 standard years (= 36,525 days). If we reckon these two periods from the date of Shem's birth (7.1.1557 in the lunar calendar, which is equivalent to 16.2.1510 in the solar calendar and 4.2.1509 in the standard calendar), we find that the alternative with 100 standard years falls on 4.2.1609 (= 11.3.1660 in the lunar calendar), i.e. corresponds exactly with the date obtained in alternative (7). The alternative with 100 solar years, on the other hand, does not yield any solution. There were in all 18 possible solutions (9 alternative dates and 2 alternatives each, as regards the time difference). Over against this, there is the requirement to find the right date. In the standard calendar there is a random chance of about 1 in 365 of hitting on a certain date. Thus 18 possible solutions give a total chance of 18/365 or about 1 in 20.[118] Nevertheless, we have found the right date, which is an indication that the proposed system corresponds to the one used in the Bible.

---

[118] Yet another variation is conceivable. The exact time of Shem's birth, according to the chronological system, was on the borderline between the 6th and the 7th days of the 1st month. It was presumed above that Shem was 100 years old on the borderline between the 26th and the 27th days of the 2nd month plus two years. But even if this event had occurred exactly one day later, the starting date could be described as the 27th day of the 2nd month and the alternative would accordingly agree with the wording of the Bible. In this way we would obtain nine more alternative dates, three of which, however, would coincide with the previous ones. Thus a total of 15 × 2 = 30 alternatives is obtained, if we take this possibility into account, i.e. the probability of reaching a solution increases to 30/365 or about *1 in 12*.

APPENDIX I 93

The second example is derived from the events surrounding the Exodus from Egypt. The actual date of the Exodus has been determined in this work with the guidance of the date of Aaron's death. According to Numbers 33.38, this took place in the 40th year after the Exodus, in the 5th month and on the 1st day of the month. The date is notable in that all the births and deaths of his ancestors ever since Arphaxad fell on the 11th day of the 3rd month in the lunar calendar (see above), according to the chronological calculation. For the sake of the symmetry one would have expected this date to have also been the date of Aaron's death.

It seems probable that the 1st day of the 5th month is the date in the solar or the standard calendar but that this date simultaneously corresponds to the 11th day of the 3rd month in the lunar calendar. The hypothesis is first tested for the solar calendar.

The only conceivable date in this context, when the 1st day of the 5th month in the solar calendar is simultaneously equivalent to the 11th day of the 3rd month in the lunar calendar, is the 11th day of the 3rd month in the year 2485 in the lunar calendar (corresponding to the 1st day of the 5th month in the year 2410 in the solar calendar). The next occasion on which this combination of dates occurs is 365 lunar years earlier or later, and is excluded for other reasons.[119]

Thus, according to the hypothesis, this was the date of Aaron's death. In this case Aaron's age of 123 years must have been reckoned in lunar years, if the date of his birth was also to fall on the 11th day of the 3rd month, i.e. it fell on the 11th day of the 3rd month in the year 2362 in the lunar calendar. The hypothesis is confirmed by the fact that this date in the solar calendar proves to coincide with the passover (the 14th day of the 1st month), a date which seems to have been specially chosen as the day of birth of the first high priest.

According to Exodus 7.7, Aaron was 83 years of age when he met Pharaoh before the Exodus and was, as already mentioned, 123 lunar years old when he died. Less than 40 lunar years must consequently

---

[119] More exactly, the event would occur, according to the hypothesis, on the borderline between the 10th and the 11th days of the 3rd month, which in the solar calendar would correspond to the borderline between the 30th day of the 4th month and the 1st day of the 5th month. If the event had occurred exactly a day later, this date could also be described as the 1st day of the 5th month and would thus agree with the wording of the Bible. In that case the combination of dates sought would thus be achieved either in the year 2318 or in the year 2683 in the lunar calendar. However, these alternatives are impossible, if we consider the framework of the chronology as a whole.

have elapsed between the Exodus and the day of his death, i.e. the information that he died in the 40th year after the Exodus must refer to lunar years. The Exodus took place on the 15th day of the 1st month. This gives three possible dates for it:

15/1 in the year 2446 in the lunar calendar
15/1 in the year 2372 in the solar calendar
(= 18/9 in the year 2445 in the lunar calendar)
15/1 in the year 2370 in the standard calendar
(= 1/5 in the year 2445 in the lunar calendar)

The information concerning Moses has been used in selecting between these three alternatives. He was 80 years of age at his meeting with Pharaoh (Ex. 7.7) and these cannot have been lunar years, since his total age of 120 years was reckoned in solar or standard years (see below) and his death occurred less than 40 solar or standard years after the Exodus (the manna, which lasted for 40 years, came to an end, as we know, more than a month after his death). Moses met Pharaoh on several occasions just before the Exodus, and the Bible does not say which occasion is referred to here (the fact that the statement occurs in close association with the second meeting is not decisive). However, (from the data given in the text) one of the meetings (the fourth) seems to have occurred 12 days before the Exodus, i.e. on the 3rd day of the 1st month. Using the second alternative for calculating the date of the Exodus, this is exactly 80 solar years after the 11th day of the 3rd month in the year 2363. With this combination Moses must also have been born on the 11th day of the 3rd month, which is a logical conclusion from the initial hypothesis. The second alternative for calculating the date of the Exodus should accordingly be chosen.

If instead the initial hypothesis had been that the date of Aaron's death (the 1st day of the 5th month) was taken from the standard calendar, this date would have coincided with the 11th day of the 3rd month in the years 2464 and 2529 in the lunar calendar. However, neither of these dates fits in with other information in the chronology.[120]

The data discussed so far thus lead to the conclusion that, reckoning by the lunar calendar, Aaron was born on 11.3.2362, that he (and Moses) had a meeting with Pharaoh 83 lunar years later or on 11.3.2445

---

[120] If the event had been displaced one day in this case also (cf. the note on the previous page), no solution would have been obtained on the whole and therefore this alternative may be neglected.

(the first meeting with Pharaoh), that Moses was born on 11.3.2363, that he (and Aaron) had a meeting with Pharaoh 80 solar years later or on 6.9 2445 and that the Exodus took place on 18.9.2445 or 15.1.2372, reckoning by the solar calendar. The solution is quite unambiguous and there seems to be no other possibility of combining the Biblical data in this calendar system.

We may test these results further, using other information. Moses died at the age of 120 years. He was more than 80 years of age at the Exodus but nevertheless wandered for more than 40 years in the wilderness (Deut. 2.7), i.e. his age of 120 years must have been reckoned in solar or standard years.

If we test the first alternative (solar years), we obtain the date of Moses' death as 3.12.2486 in the lunar calendar (more exactly, on the borderline between the 2nd and the 3rd days of the 12th month). If we add to this the 30 days of weeping and mourning (Deut. 34.8) and the six days of preparation for crossing the Jordan (Jos. 1.11, and 3.2), we find we have reached the borderline between the 9th and the 10th days of the 1st month (sunset on the 9th day). This agrees exactly with the Biblical information that Joshua told the people to sanctify themselves (Jos. 3.5); the crossing of the Jordan took place on the following day, which, according to Jos. 4.19, was the 10th day of the 1st month.

We may continue our test, using the information about the manna. This began to fall on the 15th day of the 2nd month after the Exodus (Ex. 16.1) and, as the Exodus took place on 15.1.2372 in the solar calendar (see above), the date of the first manna must have been 15.2.2372.[121] According to Jos. 5.12, the manna ceased to fall, after the crossing of the Jordan, on the 16th day of the 1st month, i.e. 16.1.2487 in the lunar calendar or 15.2.2412 in the solar calendar. Thus the people ate manna from 15.2.2372 until 15.2.2412, which agrees exactly with the statement in Ex. 16.35, that the children of Israel ate manna for 40 years. In spite of the fact that the information was taken from different passages in the Bible and from different calendars and although the dates are fixed because the date of the Exodus from Egypt was determined by the use of different and independent data, we obtain this perfect agreement.

---

[121] A displacement of one day is conceivable in this connection. It was assumed above that the children of Israel came to the wilderness of Sinai on the evening between the 14th and the 15th day. The second alternative is that they did not arrive until the 15th day itself, in which case the manna would have fallen in the night between the 15th and the 16th days. The first alternative gives exact agreement with the period of 40 years and for this reason was the one chosen.

There is another piece of interesting information as regards the manna. According to Ex. 16.26, it must have fallen for the first time on the first day of the week. If we reckon in even seven-day weeks from the beginning of the epoch, this agrees with the date given above.

The fixing of the date of the Exodus also leads to another interesting conclusion. According to Ex. 12.40, the Exodus took place on the day when the children of Israel had dwelt in Egypt for 430 years. According to Gen. 15.13, they were to be oppressed for 400 years. It has always proved difficult to fit this information into a chronological scheme. It now appears that in the system under discussion here the *total* time which the four 'important' generations (Levi, Kohath, Amram and Aaron) spent in Egypt is 430 solar years and the period of their oppression 400 lunar years (Ex. 6.16 et seq.).

What is the probability of arriving at these correspondences, if the proposed chronological system was not actually applied when these parts of the Bible were finally edited? As regards the possibility of getting the *date of Moses' birth* to fall on the 11th day of the 3rd month in the lunar calendar, it should first be noted that all Moses' meetings with Pharaoh give, broadly speaking, about 15 intervals to choose from in relation to the date of the Exodus. The Exodus, in its turn, can be assigned to three alternative days. Finally, there is the possibility that Moses' age of 80 years at the meeting was reckoned in either solar years or standard years. Altogether we have about $15 \times 3 \times 2$ possibilities and, since each possibility has a 1 in 354 chance of falling on a definite date in the lunar year, there is thus in all a 90/354 or about a 1 in 4 chance of our lighting on the right date.

As regards the *crossing of the Jordan*, there are two alternatives for determining the date of Moses' death (120 solar years or 120 standard years from the date of birth fixed above), two alternative interpretations of the time interval from the end of the days of weeping and mourning to the crossing of the Jordan and finally the possibilities that the date of the crossing (the 10th day of the 1st month) was taken from any one of the three calendars. Thus we get $2 \times 2 \times 3$ or 12 possibilities in all, each with a 1 in 354 or 365 chance of leading to the 10th day of the 1st month. Thus there is altogether about a 1 in 30 chance of lighting on the correct date.

As regards *the period of the manna*, there are two alternatives for the date on which it began, after the date of the Exodus has been determined. There is only one alternative for the date on which it ended, after the date of the crossing of the Jordan has been established. On the other hand, the period of its duration may be reckoned either in solar years or in standard years (but not in lunar years). Four possibilities give altogether only about a 1 in 90 chance that the end of the 40 years will fall on the date given in the Bible in the lunar calendar (it should be remembered that the dates of the beginning and the end are given in different calendars in the Bible). As regards the day on which the manna began, this fell on the right day of the week, as has already been mentioned, and the chance of this happening at random is 1 in 7.

All the above-mentioned correspondences will exist *simultaneously*. The random probability of this happening is obtained from the equation

$$\frac{1}{4} \times \frac{1}{30} \times \frac{1}{90} \times \frac{1}{7} = \frac{1}{75,600},$$

i.e. the chance of reaching the right conclusion in all these cases with the system of calculation employed would only have been about one in 75,000, if the system had not actually been used in editing the Bible.

The third example refers to two events connected with the Captivity in Babylon. II Kings 25.8, gives the day of Nebuzaradan's arrival as the 7th day of the 5th month, while Jer. 52.12 gives it as the 10th day of the same month. II Kings 25.27, states that the rehabilitation of Jehoiachin took place on the 27th day of the 12th month, while Jer. 52.31, states that it took place on the 25th day of the same month. Otherwise the events are described in almost identical terms, and therefore the difference in date is striking.

One of the two following hypotheses may explain the lack of agreement.

Hypothesis 1. A calendar system of the type already discussed formed the basis of the chronological information in the Bible.

Hypothesis 2. The contradictions are the work of 'chance', in the sense that they are due to scribal errors, different information from different sources, some unknown system, etc.

The consequences of Hypothesis 1 will be examined first.

According to this hypothesis, the explanation of the contradictions is that dates from different calendars were used. Are two calendars sufficient? A fact that is of importance in answering this question is that it is clear from the above-mentioned chapters that Jehoiachin's rehabilitation took place in the 26th year after Nebuzaradan's arrival in Jerusalem. In this case one date in any event cannot be taken from the lunar calendar, while the other may be taken from either the solar or the standard calendar. For the annual displacement between the lunar and the solar calendars is 11 days or 275 days in 25 years. Thus we cannot produce even approximately the same dates as are mentioned in the Bible text for the two events, by using the lunar calendar and only one other calendar.

On the other hand, it is possible that the dates in the Book of Jeremiah (the 10th day of the 5th month and the 25th day of the 12th month) were given in standard years, while those in II Kings (the 7th day of the 5th month and the 27th day of the 12th month respectively) were given in solar years. The difference of 5 days in the interval could largely be explained by the six intervening bissextile days in 25 years. However, a solution like this presupposes that the two calendars were approximately parallel at the period in question, a presupposition which was only true about the years 1461, 2922 or 4383 in the solar calendar. Even the second of these years differs by more than 300 years from the approximate date arrived at with the aid of the other data in the Bible.

Thus the remaining possibility is that all three calendars are involved. A more explicit formulation is that *one* date for each event must have been taken from the lunar calendar, since otherwise the solar and the standard calendars would have run approximately in parallel, a possibility which we may reject on the grounds given above.

There remains therefore a relatively limited number of possibilities of combining the calendars with each other. Let us assume that A denotes a time indication in the lunar calendar, B a time indication in the solar calendar and C a time indication in the standard calendar. In this case we get the following conceivable assumptions as to the calendar in which the relative date has been given:

Combination	II Kings 25.8 (7/5)	Jer. 52.12 (10/5)	II Kings 25.27 (27/12)	Jer. 52.31 (25/12)
I	A	B	A	C
II	A	B	C	A
III	A	C	A	B
IV	A	C	B	A
V	B	A	A	C
VI	B	A	C	A
VII	C	A	A	B
VIII	C	A	B	A

APPENDIX I 99

If there is a calendar system such as that assumed in Hypothesis 1, there must be a common starting date for these three calendars which, with one of the above combinations, will lead to the dates given in the respective Bible passages.

The problem may be solved in a purely mathematical way. Let us assume that 7/5 occurred after a whole years (of the type given in the respective combination), 10/5 occurred after b whole years, 17/12 after c whole years and 25/12 after d whole years. We then obtain the following two equations for combination I (the number of days from the beginning of the Biblical era to the event in question must be the same irrespective of which calendar is used).

$$\underbrace{354 \cdot a + 125}_{\text{Lunar calendar}} = \underbrace{365 \cdot b + 130}_{\text{Solar calendar}} \quad \text{(Nebuzaradan's arrival)}$$
$$\underbrace{354 \cdot c + 352}_{\text{Lunar calendar}} = \underbrace{365\tfrac{1}{4} \cdot d + 355}_{\text{Standard calendar}} \quad \text{(Jehoiachin's rehabilitation)}$$

Thus, on the left-hand side of the first equation, $354 \cdot a$ denotes the number of days in whole years and 125 the number of days from the New Year to 7/5 etc. (in the lunar calendar every other month had 30 days and the intervening months 29 days, while in the solar calendar each month had 30 days and 5 extra days were added at the end of the year).

The text also shows that the second event took place between 25 and 26 years later than the first event, i.e. $a = c - 25$ (taking into consideration that the date of the second event was later in the year than that of the first).

If b and d had been taken from the same calendar, the difference between them would also have been 25 years. However, there is a displacement between the solar and the standard calendars, which after 2922 years amounts to 2 years, after 4383 years to 3 years, etc. The time lag in the standard calendar is thus between 2 and 3 years at this point. Since d, according to the assumption in combination I, corresponds to a date in the standard clanendar at the end of the year and b to a date in the solar calendar in the middle of the year, the difference between d and b must be 22 and not 25 years. Thus, after reduction we get the following four equations:

$$354 \cdot a = 365 \cdot b + 5 \qquad (1)$$
$$354 \cdot c = 365\tfrac{1}{4} \cdot d + 3 \qquad (2)$$
$$a = c - 25 \qquad (3)$$
$$b = d - 22 \qquad (4)$$

APPENDIX I

After successive elimination we obtain the following solutions:

$$a = 3367\tfrac{177}{354} \text{ lunar years,} \qquad b = 3266 \text{ solar years,}$$
$$c = 3342\tfrac{177}{354} \text{ lunar yaers,} \qquad d = 3288 \text{ standard years.}$$

These solutions are impossible, since the prerequisite condition is that a, b, c and d must refer to *whole* years.

However, there are some further possibilities in combination I. As has already been mentioned, 7/5, for example, may denote the borderline between the 6th and the 7th days of the 5th month, the 7th day itself and finally the borderline between the 7th and the 8th days. In the same way 10/5 may mean the borderline between the 9th and the 10th days of the 5th month, the 10th day itself or the borderline between the 10th and the 11th days. If the first alternative in the first event is combined with the last in the second, we get a difference of 6 days in equation (1) instead of 5. If we reverse the combinations, we get a difference of 4 days. This gives three alternatives in equation (1) and three in equation (2). Thus, while we have difference of 2 surplus days between equations (1) and (2), according to the wording, we may use all the combinations to obtain differences of 0, 1, 2, 3 and 4 days. The following combinations can be shown to be possible:

Difference in days between equations (1) and (2)	May be combined with the following differences in days *within* equation (1)
0	4
1	4, 5
2	4, 5, 6
3	5, 6
4	6

Total: 9 combinations

However, in this case none of the combinations leads to even numbers of a etc. The solutions are not possible and therefore we have to pass on to the testing of main combination II (ABCA). For this we obtain in a similar fashion the following four equations:

APPENDIX I

$$354 \cdot a + 125 = 365 \cdot b + 130$$
$$365\tfrac{1}{4} \cdot c + 357 = 354 \cdot d + 350$$
$$a = d - 25$$
$$b = c - 22$$

If we solve this system of equations, we find that $a = 3351\tfrac{1}{354}$, i.e. the solution is not possible. If, however, 7/5 is interpreted as the borderline between the 7th and 8th days of the 5th month, 10/5 as the borderline between the 9th and the 10th days, 25/12 as the borderline between the 25th and the 26th days of the 12th month and finally 27/12 as the borderline between the 26th and the 27th days, i.e. both the events are assigned to the time of sunset, we obtain, on the one hand, two sharply defined starting-points (a fact to which importance was probably attached when the chronological system in question was drawn up) and, on the other, a solution which satisfies all the conditions. This solution is

$a = 3351$ lunar years, $\qquad b = 3250$ solar years,
$c = 3272$ standard years, $\qquad d = 3376$ lunar years

i.e. the solution given in the present work, although the author's calculation was made in a different way.

Similar calculations were made for all the other main combinations and their sub-alternatives. None of the solutions fulfilled the condition that a, b, c and d must be whole numbers. The solutions obtained for the first event expressed in lunar years (a or b) in the sub-alternative which corresponds to the exact text of the Bible are as follows:

Comb.	I	II	III	IV	V	VI	VII	VIII
a or b	$3367\tfrac{177}{354}$	$3351\tfrac{1}{354}$	$4139\tfrac{182}{354}$	$4156\tfrac{8}{345}$	$3342\tfrac{261}{354}$	$3326\tfrac{85}{354}$	$4164\tfrac{92}{354}$	$4180\tfrac{272}{354}$

From these solutions, alternatives nos. III, IV, VII and VIII must be rejected on general grounds, since the other chronological information given in the Bible excludes the possibility that the starting-point of the chronology should be so long before the events in question. Thus, only four conceivable main combinations remain, each with nine sub-alternatives. There are accordingly 36 possibilities in all. Since the lunar year has 354 days, there is a random probability of 1 in 354 that a solution for a etc. will yield a whole number of years. Thus 36 alternatives have a random chance of about *1 in 10* of leading to a solution. Nevertheless, a solution was obtained that satisfied all the conditions and in addition proved to fit in detail into the chronological framework which emerged from the other dates given in the Bible. Thus, mathematically speaking, the calculation shows that Hypothesis 1 is considerably more probable than Hypothesis 2, even though its only support consisted of the above-mentioned four dates, besides which the calculation gives an exact and unambiguous interval between the starting-point of the chronological system and the events in question.

As has already been shown, however, the probability of the system is increased by the fact that it leads to a solution in other cases as well. Since the dates of all the events discussed in this Appendix must agree *simultaneously* with the stated conditions, we may calculate the combined probability of these conditions being fulfilled. This probability was about 1 in 12 in the first example, about 1 in 75,000 in the second and about 1 in 10 in the third. Thus, the chance of these conditions being fulfilled simultaneously is

$$\frac{1}{12} \times \frac{1}{75,000} \times \frac{1}{10} = \frac{1}{9,000,000},$$

i.e. only *one chance in nearly 10 million*.

The above calculation shows the order of magnitude concerned here but must not be taken as an exact calculation. On the one hand, it is conceivable that, on the basis of the Bible wording etc., a further possibility may be concocted, as regards one event or another. On the other hand, no great regard was paid in the above calculation to the condition that not only the date but also the *year* must fit into the wider context. To be sure, some alternatives were rejected, as they clearly did not coincide with the date arrived at on other grounds. But, over and above this, there were in some cases narrow limits for the location of the event in time, and these restrictions were disregarded in the above calculation. Presumably the random probability that all the conditions could be fulfilled was for this reason much less than that calculated above.

This calculation, using dates from only three sections of the Biblical chronology, shows that the only reasonable explanation of the correspondences found is that the proposed system actually was used in the editing of the sections of the Old Testament in question. This conclusion is naturally confirmed to a very large extent by the fact that there is also a similar correspondence as regards other sections and that certain basic dates give rise to peculiar combinations of figures or reveal hidden connections with sacred feasts and the like.

APPENDIX II

TABLES

The line numbers on the right in the tables are the numbers of the events in question and correspond to the description of the events in the text. The column in the left-hand margin of the tables gives the number of the days from "the beginning". When just one number is given, this means that the event happened when so many *full* days had passed (and accordingly happened at the end of the day, at sunset). The three middle columns give the date in the lunar, solar and standard calendars respectively (cf., p. 8). For example, 15.7.3606 means the 15th day of the 7th month in the 3606th year. The complete tables are found in Stenring: *The Enclosed Garden*.

APPENDIX II

No of days from "the beginning".	"Lunar" calendar ☽	"Solar" calendar ☉	"Standard" calendar ✶	Line no
0	1.1.1	1.1.1	1.1.1	−1
6	6–7.1.1	7.1.1	7.1.1	−2
46,026	7.1.131	7.2.127	6.1.127	−3
83,196	7.1.236	12.12.228	16.10.228	−4
115,056	7.1.326	22.3.316	4.1.316	−5
139,836	7.1.396	12.2.384	12.11.383	−6
162,846	7.1.461	27.2.447	11.11.446	−7
220,194	7.1.623	10.4.604	15.11.603	−8
243,204	7.1.688	25.4.667	14.11.666	−9
309,402	7.1.875	8.9.848	7.2.848	−10
329,226	7.1.931	2.13.902	17.5.902	−11
349,404	7.1.988	10.4.958	16.8.957	−12
368,874	7.1.1043	15.8.1011	8.12.1010	−13
373,830	7.1.1057	11.3.1025	1.7.1024	−14
403,566	7.1.1141	2.9.1106	1.12.1105	−15
437,196	7.1.1236	22.10.1198	28.12.1197	−16
456,666	7.1.1291	22.2.1252	15.4.1251	−17
503,394	7.1.1423	30.2.1380	21.3.1379	−18
550,830	7.1.1557	16.2.1510	4.2.1509	−19
584,460	7.1.1652	6.4.1602	1.3.1601	−20
586,230	7.1.1657	11.2.1607	5.1.1606	−21
586,263	10.2.1657	14.3.1607	8.2.1606	−22
586,270	17.2.1657	21.3.1607	15.2.1606	−23
586,310	28.3.1657	1.5.1607	25.3.1606	−24
586,420	20.7.1657	21.8.1607	15.7.1606	−25
586,422–3	22.7.1657	23.8.1607	17.7.1606	−26
586,490	1.10.1657	1.11.1607	25.9.1606	−27
586,530	12.11.1657	11.12.1607	5.11.1606	−28
586,531	13.11.1657	12.12.1607	6.11.1606	−29
586,561	13.12.1657	7.1.1608	6.12.1606	−30
586,562	14.12.1657	8.1.1608	7.12.1606	−31
586,569	21.12.1657	15.1.1608	14.12.1606	−32
586,570	22.12.1657	16.1.1608	15.12.1606	−33
586,577	29.12.1657	23.1.1608	22.12.1606	−34
586,578	1.1.1658	24.1.1608	23.12.1606	−35
586,647	11.3.1658	3.4.1608	27.2.1607	−37
587,355	11.3.1660	11.3.1610	4.2.1609	−38
599,745	11.3.1695	21.2.1644	6.1.1643	−39
610,365	11.3.1725	26.3.1673	4.2.1672	−40

APPENDIX II

	Line nr
Line number one signifies Era Mundus	−1
Adam and Eve. Six days from line 1 (Gen. 1.31, 2.2).	−2
Birth of Seth (Gen. 5.3)	−3
Birth of Enos (Gen. 5.6)	−4
Birth of Cainan (Gen. 5.9)	−5
Birth of Mahalaleel (Gen. 5.12)	−6
Birth of Jared (Gen. 5.15). Line number 7 is 65 ☽ years from line 6.	−7
Birth of Enoch (Gen. 5.18)	−8
Birth of Methuselah (Gen. 5.21)	−9
Birth of Lamech (Gen. 5.25)	−10
Death of Adam, Seth head of mankind (Gen. 5.4–5)	−11
Translation of Enoch.	−12
Death of Seth. Enos head of mankind	−13
Birth of Noah (Gen. 5.28)	−14
Death of Enos. Cainan head of mankind (Gen. 5.10–11).	−15
Death of Cainan. Mahalaleel head of mankind (Gen. 5.13–14)	−16
Death of Mahalaleel. Jared head of mankind (Gen. 5.16–17)	−17
Death of Jared. Methuselah head of mankind (Gen. 5.19–20)	−18
Birth of Shem (Gen. 5.32). Line 19 is 500 ☽ years from line 14	−19
Death of Lamech (Gen. 5.30–31)	20
Death of Metuselah. Noah head of mankind at the age of 600 ☽ years	21
The message (Gen. 7.1,)	−22
'The windows of heaven were opened' (Gen. 7.10–11)	−23
The windows of heaven are closed (Gen. 7.12). Line 24 is 40 days from line 23.	−24
The fountains of the great deep cease to rise. The waters begin to return from off the earth (Gen. 7.24, 8.3). Line 24 is 40 + 70 days from line 25, and line 25 represents the point of equilibrium between the time when the tops of the mountains disappeared and the time when the tops of the mountains were seen again. The mountains were below the surface of the water for 140 days (70 + 70). The dates of the beginning of the first and the last days of the future 'spring' festival are to be found 120 ☽ years before the tops of the mountains disappeared below the surface (Gen. 6.3).	−25
The Ark rests upon the mountains of Ararat (Gen. 8.4)	−26
The tops of the mountains are seen (Gen. 8.5). Line 27 is 70 days from line 25.	−27
A raven is sent forth (Gen. 8.6–7). Line 28 is 40 days from line 27	−28
The raven was expected to return at sunset but did not return	−29
A dove is sent forth 30 days from line 29	−30
The dove returns at sunset one day from line 30	−31
A dove is sent forth seven days from line 31	−32
The dove returns at sunset one day from line 32	−33
A dove is sent forth seven days from line 33	−34
The dove was expected to return at sunset—one day from line 34—but she did not return. The waters had returned from off the earth, and Noah removed the covering of the Ark (Gen. 8.13)	−35
The earth is once more dry (Gen. 8.14).	−37
Birth of Arphachshad (Gen. 11.10). 100 ☆ years from line 19. Line 38 is two ☽ years from line 37	−38
Birth of Salah. (Gen. 11.12)	−39
Birth of Eber (Gen. 11.14). Line 40 is 65 ☽ years or 63 ☆ years from line 38.	−40

APPENDIX II

	☽	☉	✷	
622,401	11.3.1759	17.3.1706	16.1.1705	−41
633,021	11.3.1789	22.4.1735	14.2.1734	−42
644,349	11.3.1821	5.5.1766	19.2.1765	−43
654,969	11.3.1851	10.6.1795	17.3.1794	−44
665,235	11.3.1880	26.7.1823	26.4.1822	−45
690,015	11.3.1950	16.6.1891	29.2.1890	−46
693,201	11.3.1959	7.3.1900	23.11.1898	−47
707,007	11.3.1998	3.1.1938	10.9.1936	−48
707,361	11.3.1999	27.12.1938	28.8.1937	−49
710,547	11.3.2008	18.9.1947	17.5.1946	−50
716,565	11.3.2025	11.3.1964	11.11.1962	−51
717,627	11.3.2028	8.2.1967	7.10.1965	−52
720,105	11.3.2035	26.11.1973	19.7.1972	−53
720,459	11.3.2036	15.11.1974	7.7.1973	−54
725,061	11.3.2049	22.6.1987	11.2.1986	−55
725,415	11.3.2050	11.6.1988	30.1.1987	−56
725,769	11.3.2051	30.5.1989	19.1.1988	−57
737,805	11.3.2085	21.5.2022	1.1.2021	−58
738,159	11.3.2086	10.5.2023	25.12.2021	−59
739,575	11.3.2090	26.3.2027	10.11.2025	−60
742,407	11.3.2098	3.13.2034	10.8.2033	−61
746,655	11.3.2110	21.8.2046	25.3.2045	−62
751,965	11.3.2125	6.3.2061	12.10.2059	−63
753,027	11.3.2128	3.2.2064	8.9.2062	−64
760,815	11.3.2150	6.6.2085	1.1.2084	−65
768,957	11.3.2173	28.9.2107	17.4.2106	−66
769,980	1.2.2176	16.7.2110	4.2.2109	−67
774,621	11.3.2189	2.4.2123	22.10.2121	−68
775,329	11.3.2191	10.3.2125	30.9.2123	−69
775,359	11.4.2191	10.4.2125	30.10.2123	−70
777,807	11.3.2198	28.12.2131	11.7.2130	−71
777,814	18.3.2198	5.13.2131	18.7.2130	−72
778,869	11.3.2201	25.11.2134	7.6.2133	−73
780,285	11.3.2205	11.10.2138	22.4.2137	−74
789,135	11.3.2230	6.1.2163	16.7.2161	−78
790,905	11.3.2235	16.11.2167	20.5.2166	−79
792,675	11.3.2240	21.9.2172	24.3.2171	−80
793,383	11.3.2242	29.8.2174	1.3.2173	−81
794,105	25.3.2244	21.8.2176	23.2.2175	−83
794,119–20	9.4.2244	5.9.2176	7.3.2175	−84
800,310	5.10.2261	21.8.2193	19.2.2192	−85
800,817	11.3.2263	8.1.2195	10.7.2193	−86
801,468–9	13.1.2265	24.10.2196	21.4.2195	−87
819,225	11.3.2315	16.6.2245	6.12.2243	−88
827,367	11.3.2338	8.10.2267	17.3.2266	−89
835,863	11.3.2362	14.1.2291	22.6.2289	−90

APPENDIX II

Birth of Peleg (Gen. 11.16)	−41
Birth of Reu (Gen. 11.18)	−42
Birth of Serug (Gen. 11.20)	−43
Birth of Nahor (Gen. 11.22)	−44
Birth of Terah (Gen. 11.24)	−45
Birth of Abram (Gen. 11.26)	46
Birth of Sarai (Sarah) (Gen. 17.17)	−47
Death of Peleg (Gen. 11.19)	−48
Death of Nahor (Gen. 11.25)	−49
Death of Noah (Gen. 9.28–29)	−50
Abram departed out of Haran (Gen. 12.4). Line 51 is 365 ☽ years or 354 ☉ years from line 38. Line 51 is 75 ☽ years from line 46.	−51
Death of Reu (Gen. 11.21)	−52
Abram takes Hagar to wife (Gen. 16.3)	−53
Birth of Ishmael (Gen. 16.16)	−54
The covenant (Gen. 17.1)	−55
Birth of Isaac (Gen. 17.21, 21.5)	−56
Death of Serug (Gen. 11.23)	−57
Death of Terah (Gen. 11.32). Turn of the year in the ✶ calendar.	−58
Death of Sarah (Gen. 23.1)	−59
Isaac takes Rebekah to wife (Gen. 25.20)	−60
Death of Arphachshad. Gen. 11.13.	−61
Births of Esau and Jacob (Gen. 25.26)	−62
Death of Abraham (Gen. 25.7)	−63
Death of Salah (Gen. 11.15)	−64
Esau takes to wife Bashemath and Judith (Gen. 26.34)	−65
Death of Ishmael (Gen. 25.17)	−66
Death of Shem (Gen. 11.11), Eber head of mankind	−67
Death of Eber (Gen. 11.17). Isaac head of mankind	−68
Jacob meets Rachel	−69
The agreement between Laban and Jacob (= Israel) (Gen. 29.14–18)	−70
Jacob takes Leah to wife (Gen. 29.20–25)	−71
Jacob takes Rachel to wife (Gen. 29.28–31)	−72
Birth of Levi (Gen. 29.34). Judah and Dan were born one ☽ year after Levi, and the wheat harvest began 40 weeks after the birth of Judah. Naphtali was born one ☽ year after the birth of Judah; Gad and Asher (twins), and Issachar one ☽ year after Naphtali. Leah said her prayers 40 weeks before the birth of Issachar.	−73
Birth of Zebulun and Dinah (twins), and Joseph 4 ☽ years from line 73. Ten children were born in four years (Gen. 30.23–24). Compare Plato's *Kritias* (in the middle of that dialogue)	−74
Death of Isaac, head of mankind (Gen. 27, Gen. 35.28)	−78
Joseph interprets Pharaoh's dreams (Gen. 41.46)	−79
Birth of Kohath	−80
The first year of famine (the beginning) (Gen. 41.54)	−81
Jacob before Pharaoh (Gen. 45.9, 45.19, 46.5, 47.9)	−83
Israel settles in Rameses in Goshen	−84
Death of Jacob (Gen. 47.28)	−85
Birth of Amram; at the age of 100 ☽ years Amram begets Moses	−86
The time of affliction begins.	−87
Death of Joseph (Gen. 50.22)	−88
Death of Levi (Ex. 6.16)	−89
Birth of Aaron	−90

108 APPENDIX II

	☽	☉	✶	
836,217	11.3.2363	3.1.2292	11.6.2290	−91
839,757	11.3.2373	18.9.2301	19.2.2300	−92
849,315	11.3.2400	26.11.2327	20.4.2326	−93
851,135–6	2.5.2405	21.11.2332	14.4.2331	−94
865,245	11.3.2445	16.7.2371	4.12.2369	−95
865,417	6.9.2445	3.1.2372	21.5.2370	−98
865,428	17.9.2445	14.1.2372	2.6.2370	−99
865,429–30	18.9.2445	15.1.2372	3.6.2370	−100
865,459	18.10.2445	15.2.2372	3.7.2370	101
865,459–60	18.10.2445	15.2.2372	3.7.2370	−102
865,475	5.11.2445	1.3.2372	19.7.2370	−103
865,475–6	5.11.2445	1.3.2372	19.7.2370	−104
865,476–7	6.11.2445	2.3.2372	20.7.2370	−105
865,477–8	7.11.2445	3.3.2372	21.7.2370	−106
865,478–9	8.11.2445	4.3.2372	22.7.2370	−107
865,483–4	13.11.2445	9.3.2372	27.7.2370	−108
865,523–4	23.12.2445	19.4.2372	7.9.2370	−109
865,524–5	24.12.2445	20.4.2372	8.9.2370	−110
865,525–6	25.12.2445	21.4.2372	9.9.2370	−111
865,565–6	6.2.2446	1.6.2372	19.10.2370	−112
865,642–3	24.4.2446	18.8.2372	1.1.2371	−114
865,655–6	8.5.2446	1.9.2372	14.1.2371	−116
865,672–3	25.5.2446	18.9.2372	1.2.2371	−117
865,691–2	14.6.2446	7.10.2372	20.2.2371	−118
865,745–6	9.8.2446	1.12.2372	14.4.2371	−119
865,785–6	20.9.2446	6.1.2373	24.5.2371	−120
866,065–6	5.7.2447	16.10.2373	29.2.2372	−121
879,405	11.3.2485	1.5.2410	10.9.2408	−123
879,945–6	20.9.2486	26.10.2411	29.2.2410	−126
879,979–80	24.10.2486	30.11.2411	3.4.2410	−127
879,985–6	1.11.2486	6.12.2411	9.4.2410	−128
880,017	3.12.2486	3.1.2412	11.5.2410	−129
880,047	4.1.2487	3.2.2412	11.6.2410	−131
880,053–4	10.1.2487	9.2.2412	17.6.2410	−132
880,057	14.1.2487	13.2.2412	21.6.2410	−133

APPENDIX II

Birth of Moses	−91
Death of Kohath (Ex. 6.18)	−92
Death of Amram (Ex. 6.20)	−93
Birth of Caleb (Jos. 14.7–10)	−94
Moses and Aaron before Pharaoh (Ex. 5.1, 7.7)	−95
Moses and Aaron before Pharaoh (Ex. 7.7, 8.1–9). Seven days earlier, the beginning of the five unlucky epagomenal days (the last five days of the year) had put a temporary stop to the animated conferences between Moses and Pharaoh	−98
The day of passover. (Ex. 12.6, Deut. 16.1–6)	−99
Exodus. Israel leaves Rameses in Goshen at midnight. From the first settlement in Rameses (line 84) a total of 430 ☉ years has elapsed. These years are the years of the lives of Levi, Kohath, Amram, and Aaron put together. To these four generations, 400 ☽ years have elapsed from the beginning of the affliction (line 87) (Gen. 15.13, Ex. 12.2, 12.40, 13.4, Deut. 16.1, 16.6)	−100
Sin is reached at sunset at the beginning of the first day of the seven-day week (Ex. 16.1)	−101
Manna is gathered in the morning (Ex. 16.13–15, Ex. 16.35)	−102
Sinai is reached (Ex. 19.1)	−103
Moses' first ascent of the mountain and his descent (Ex. 19.3)	−104
The people are sanctified and told to be ready	−105
Moses' second ascent of the mountain. Smoke on the mountain	−106
Moses builds an altar at the foot of the mountain. The seventy elders	−107
A voice calls to Moses out of the midst of the cloud. The beginning of a period of 40 days (Ex. 24.16–18, Deut. 9.9)	−108
Moses' descent from the mountain. The golden calf	−109
Moses' fourth ascent of the mountain and his descent	−110
Moses' fifth ascent of the mountain. Two unwritten tables. The beginning of a period of 40 days (Deut. 9.18, 9.25)	−111
Moses' descent from Mount Sinai 90 (= 3 × 30) days after his first ascent of the mountain	−112
The tabernacle is erected (Ex. 40.17)	−114
The beginning of the day of passover (Num. 9.1–5). 180 (= 6 × 30) days from line 103	−116
The census (Num. 1.1)	−177
Sinai is abandoned (Num. 10.11)	−118
Spies are sent out from Paran in Kadesh. (Num. 13.21, 13.26–27). Line 119 is 40 ☆ years from line 94 and 270 (= 9 × 30) days from line 104	−119
The return of the spies (Num. 13.26). Line 120 is 40 days from line 119. Num. 14.33–35	−120
Kadesh is abandoned 40 weeks from line 120	−121
Death of Aaron (Num. 33.38–39). 123 ☽ years from line 90	−123
The desert is abandoned. Zered. Inhabited land (Num. 14.33, 32.9–13, Deut. 2.13–14, Jos. 5.6). Line 126 is 40 ☽ years from line 120 and 38 ☆ years from line 121	−126
Israel's first settlement in Heshbon east of Jordan (Num. 21.13, 32.9–13, Deut. 2.7, 2.13–14, Jos. 5.6)	−127
Moses' great speech to the people (Deut. 1.3). Line 128 is 6 days from line 127 and 40 days from line 126	−128
Death of Moses (Deut. 31.2, 34.7). 120 ☉ years from line 91	−129
End of the days of weeping (Deut. 34.8)	−131
Israel passes over Jordan (Jos. 3.15, 4.19)	−132
Beginning of the day of passover in the ☽ calendar (Jos. 5.10)	−133

APPENDIX II

	☽	☉	✶	
880,059–60	16.1.2487	15.2.2412	23.6.2410	−135
882,181–2	14.1.2493	12.12.2417	14.4.2416	−136
884,770–1	7.5.2500	11.1.2425	16.5.2423	−137
887,602–3	7.5.2508	18.10.2432	16.2.2431	−138
901,762–3	7.5.2548	3.8.2471	26.11.2469	−139
908,134–5	7.5.2566	15.1.2489	4.5.2487	−140
936,454–5	7.5.2646	20.8.2566	20.11.2564	−141
943,534–5	7.5.2666	10.1.2586	5.4.2584	−142
957,694–5	7.5.2706	30.10.2624	10.1.2623	−143
960,172–3	7.5.2713	13.8.2631	26.10.2629	−144
973,270–1	7.5.2750	1.7.2667	5.9.2665	−145
974,332–3	7.5.2753	28.5.2670	2.8.2668	−146
975,394–5	7.5.2756	25.4.2673	28.6.2671	−147
975,748–9	7.5.2757	14.4.2674	17.6.2672	−148
983,536–7	7.5.2779	17.8.2695	14.10.2693	−149
989,554–5	7.5.2796	10.2.2712	3.4.2710	−150
989,908–9	7.5.2797	29.1.2713	22.3.2711	−151
992,032–3	7.5.2803	28.11.2718	14.1.2717	−152
993,802–3	7.5.2808	3.10.2723	23.11.2721	−153
994,510–1	7.5.2810	11.9.2725	1.11.2723	−154
998,050–1	7.5.2820	21.5.2735	8.7.2733	−155
1,000,882–3	7.5.2828	23.2.2743	8.4.2741	−156
1,007,962–3	7.5.2848	18.7.2762	29.8.2760	−157
1,008,172–3	10.12.2848	13.2.2763	23.3.2761	−158
1,008,180–1	18.12.2848	21.2.2763	1.4.2761	−159
1,013,435–6	22.10.2863	16.7.2777	23.8.2775	−160
1,015,042–3	7.5.2868	13.12.2781	14.1.2780	−161
1,015,050–1	15.5.2868	21.12.2781	22.1.2780	−162
1,015,260–1	18.12.2868	16.7.2782	22.8.2780	163
1,023,655–6	6.9.2892	16.7.2805	16.8.2803	−164
1,024,205–6	25.3.2894	16.1.2807	15.2.2805	−165
1.024,385–6	28.9.2894	16.7.2807	15.8.2805	−166
1,026,940–1	16.12.2901	16.7.2814	14.8.2812	−167
1,034,970–1	22.8.2924	16.7.2836	8.8.2834	−169
1,038,985–6	25.12.2935	16.7.2847	5.8.2845	−170
1,040,437–8	2.2.2940	8.7.2851	26.7.2849	−171
1,042,992–3	20.4.2947	8.7.2858	25.7.2856	−172

APPENDIX II 111

Manna ceases to fall in the morning (Jos. 5.12). Line 135 is 40 ☉ years from line 102 . . . . –135
The division of the land west of Jordan (the land of Canaan) (Jos. 14.6–10). Line 136 is 45 ⚹ years from line 119. . . . . –136
The beginning of the oppression under the Mesopotamians (Jud. 3.8) . . . –137
The people are rescued by Othniel (Jud. 3.9–11) . . . . –138
The beginning of the oppression under the Moabites (Jud. 3.14) . . . . . –139
The people are rescued by Ehud. . . . . –140
The beginning of the oppression under the Canaanites (Jud. 4.3) . . . . . –141
The people are rescued by Deborah and Barak (Jud. 5.31) . . . . –142
The beginning of the oppression under the Midianites (Jud. 6.1). . . . . –143
The people are rescued by Gideon (Jud. 8.28) . . . . –144
Birth of Eli. . . . . –145
Abimelech king (Jud. 9.22) . . . . –146
Tola judge (Jud. 10.2) . . . . –147
Tola and Jair judges (Jud. 10.3) . . . . –148
The beginning of the oppression under the Amorites (Jud. 10.8). . . . . –149
Jephtah's message to the king of the Amorites. 300 ⚹ years from line 127 and 17 ☽ years from line 149 (Jud. 11.26) . . . . –150
The people are rescued by Jephtah (Jud. 12.7). . . . . –151
Ibzan judge (Jud. 12.9). . . . . –152
Eli judge in the south-west . . . . –153
Elon judge (Jud. 12.11). . . . . –154
Abdon judge (Jud. 12.14). . . . . –155
The beginning of the oppression under the Philistines (Jud. 13.1) . . . . –156
The Ark is taken by the Philistines. Samson judge in the south-west (Jud. 13–16, I Sam. 4.15–18) . . . . –157
The Philistines come to a decision about the Ark 210 days (= 7 months) from line 157 (I Sam. 6.1, 6.12–13, 7.1–2) . . . . –158
The day after the end of the wheat harvest the people of Beth-Shemesh come to a decision about the Ark; 8 days from line 158. . . . . –159
David born . . . . –160
Samuel sacrifices a lamb on the day of the passover, the advancing Philistines are scattered and the oppression ceases 20 ☽ years from line 157 (Jud. 15.20, 16.31, I Sam. 7.9–10). . . . . –161
Saul, the king-to-be, is anointed in the morning; eight days and a half from the beginning of the day of the passover, i.e. seven days and a half from the beginning of the Feast of the Unleavened Bread (1 Sam. 9–10, Ex. 23.15) . . –162
Saul made king 20 ☽ years from line 159 and seven months from line 162 (I Sam. 7.2, I Sam. 11-13) . . . . –163
Saul's death. . . . . –164
David king of Judah in Hebron (Ish-bosheth is still living) . . . . –165
David king of all Israel in Hebron (Ish-bosheth is dead) . . . . –166
David king of all Israel in Jerusalem. 7 ☉ years from line 166 . . . . . . –167
Solomon made king. 22 ☉ years from line 167 . . . . –169
David's death; Solomon head of the royal house 40 ☉ years from line 166 and 11 ☉ years from line 169 (II Sam. 5.4–5, I Sam. 27.7, 28.19, II Sam. 1.1–2, 2.4, 2.10–11, 3.2–5, 4.5, 6.11, 14.28, 15.7, 21.1, I Ki. 2.11) . . . . –170
The Temple foundations laid in the morning on the second day of Zif (Zif is the second month in the ☽ year) (I Ki. 6.1, 6.37, II Chr. 3.2). . . . . . . –171
The beginning of the consecration of the altar. In the morning. 7 ☉ years from line 171 (I Ki 8.2, 8.65–66). . . . . –172

	☽	☉	✶	
1,042,999	27.4.2947	15.7.2858	2.8.2856	−173
1,043,007	6.5.2947	23.7.2858	10.8.2856	−174
1,049,570–1	20.11.2965	16.7.2876	28.7.2874	−175
1,049,737–8	10.5.2966	3.13.2876	10.1.2875	−176
1,049,740	13.5.2966	1.1.2877	13.1.2875	−177
1,049,964	1.1.2967	15.8.2877	27.8.2875	−178
1,050,836	17.6.2969	2.1.2880	13.1.2878	−179
1,053,027	25.8.2975	3.1.2886	13.1.2884	−180
1,054,123	30.9.2978	4.1.2889	13.1.2887	−181
1,055,949	27.11.2983	5.1.2894	13.1.2892	−182
1,057,045	2.1.2987	6.1.2897	13.1.2895	−183
1,057,410	13.1.2988	6.1.2898	13.1.2896	−184
1,057,776	25.1.2989	7.1.2899	13.1.2897	−185
1,058,141	6.2.2990	7.1.2900	13.1.2898	−186
1,061,428	19.5.2999	9.1.2909	13.1.2907	−187
1,062,159	12.6.3001	10.1.2911	13.1.2909	−188
1,062,221	15.8.3001	12.3.2911	15.3.2909	−189
1.065,811	6.10.3011	12.1.2921	13.1.2919	−190
1,066,176	17.10.3012	12.1.2922	13.1.2920	191
1,066,907	11.11.3014	13.1.2924	13.1.2922	−192
1,066,914	18.11.3014	20.1.2924	20.1.2922	−193
1,068,368	26.12.3018	14.1.2928	13.1.2926	−194
1,068,733	8.1.3020	14.1.2929	13.1.2927	−195
1,070,559	5.3.3025	15.1.2934	13.1.2932	−196
1,071,290	28.3.3027	16.1.2936	13.1.2934	−197
1,072,020	20.4.3029	16.1.2938	13.1.2936	−198
1,073,116	25.5.3032	17.1.2941	13.1.2939	−199
1,073,481	6.6.3033	17.1.2942	13.1.2940	−200
1,076,769	20.9.3042	20.1.2951	13.1.2949	−201
1,079,325	9.12.3049	21.1.2958	13.1.2956	−202

APPENDIX II   113

The beginning of the Feast of Tabernacles in the ☉ calendar. Sunset at the
beginning of the second day in the month of Bul (the 8th month) . . . . –173
Sunset at the end of the Sabbath which immediately follows the Feast of
Tabernacles. On the 23rd day of the 7th month Solomon sent the people away
to their tents (II Chr. 7.8–10) . . . . –174
Solomon's death; the beginning of the interregnum, 40 ☉ years from line
169 and 29 ☉ years from line 170 . . . . –175
The first assembly . . . . –176
The second assembly; Rehoboam, king of Judah. Jeroboam I, king of
Israel in the camp, (I Ki. 12.12) . . . . –177
The beginning of the feast of Jeroboam (I Ki. 12.32-33) . . . . –178
Abijah (Abijam) made king of Judah 3 ☾ years from line 177 . . . . . . –179
Asa made king of Judah 6 ☾ years from line 179 . . . . –180
Jehoshaphat of Judah born 3 ☾ years from line 180 . . . . –181
Rehoboam's death; Abijah (Abijam) head of the royal house of Judah 8 ☾
years from line 180 (I Ki. 14.21, 15.1–2, II Chr. 12.13, 13.1) . . . . –182
Abijah's (Abijam's) death; Asa head of the royal house of Judah 3 ☾ years
from line 182 (I Ki. 15.9–10, II Chr. 13.2) . . . . –183
Nadab king of Israel in Tirzah one ☾ year from line 183 (I Ki. 15.25) . . . –184
Jeroboam's death; Nadab head of the royal house of Israel one ☾ year from
line 184 (I Ki. 14.20). . . . . –185
Nadab's death; Baasha king of Israel in Tirzah one ☾ year from line 185 . . –186
Jehoram, the son of Jehoshaphat of Judah, is born . . . . –187
Zerah is conquered by Asa 11 ☾ years from line 186. Line 188 marks the
beginning of a period of peace lasting for 10 ☾ years . . . . –188
The beginning of the feast of Asa (II Chr. 15.10). . . . . –189
Baasha comes up against Judah 10 ☾ years from line 188 . . . . –190
Elah made king of Israel in Tirzah one ☾ year from line 190 (I Ki. 16.8) . . –191
Jehoshaphat made king of Judah; Baasha's death; Elah's death; Zimri
king of Israel in Tirzah; Tibni king of Israel in Tirzah; Omri king of Israel
in the camp. Two ☾ years from line 191 (I Ki. 16.10, 16.15) . . . . . . –192
Zimri's death; Tibni sole king in Tirzah 7 days from line 192 . . . . . . –193
Tibni's death; Omri king of Israel takes up his residence in Tirzah. 4 ☾
years from line 192. . . . . –194
Ahaziah, the son of Jehoram of Judah, is born one ☾ year from line 194. . –195
Omri, king of Israel, takes up his residence in Samaria; Ahab made king of
Israel in Tirzah 6 ☾ years from line 194. . . . . –196
Omri's death; Ahab, king of Israel, takes up his residence in Samaria;
Jehoram, the son of Ahab, made king of Israel in Tirzah two ☾ years from
line 196 . . . . –197
Asa's death; Jehoshaphat head of the royal house of Judah two ☾ years
from line 197 (I Ki. 22.41, II Chr. 16.13). . . . . –198
Jehoram, the son of Jehoshaphat, made king of Judah; Ahaziah, the son of
Ahab, made king of Israel in Samaria 3 ☾ years from line 198 (II Ki. 8.16) –199
Ahaziah of Samaria is seriously hurt and confined to bed for the rest of his
life; Jehoram, king of Israel, takes up his residence in Samaria; Tirzah ceases
to be seat of government one ☾ year from line 199 (II Ki. 1.2, 1.17, 3.1) . . –200
Ahaziah, the son of Jehoram of Judah, made king of Judah 9 ☾ years from
line 200 . . . . –201
Ahab's death. Ahaziah and Jehoram, the sons of Ahab, are co-regents of
Israel in Samaria 7 ☾ years from line 201 and 16 ☾ years from line 200
(I Ki. 16.29, 22.40). . . . . –202

	☽	☉	✶	
1,080,056	3.1.3052	22.1.2960	13.1.2958	−203
1,081,152	7.2.3055	23.1.2963	13.1.2961	−204
1,084,074	9.5.3063	25.1.2971	13.1.2969	−205
1,084,439	20.5.3064	25.1.2972	13.1.2970	−206
1.086,630	28.7.3070	26.1.2978	13.1.2976	−207
1,092,109	20.1.3086	30.1.2993	13.1.2991	−208
1,093,570	6.3.3090	1.2.2997	13.1.2995	−209
1,094,666	10.4.3093	2.2.3000	13.1.2998	−210
1,097,953	23.7.3102	4.2.3009	13.1.3007	−211
1,098,684	16.8.3104	5.2.3011	13.1.3009	−212
1,099,779	20.9.3107	5.2.3014	13.1.3012	−213
1,101,240	6.11.3111	6.2.3018	13.1.3016	−214
1,103,432	15.1.3118	8.2.3024	13.1.3022	−215
1,103,797	26.1.3119	8.2.3025	13.1.3023	−216
1,104,738	23.9.3121	9.9.3027	13.8.3025	−217
1,109,276	18.7.3134	12.2.3040	13.1.3038	−218
1,114,599	1.8.3149	15.9.3054	13.8.3052	−219
1,118,407	4.5.3160	18.2.3065	13.1.3063	−220
1,118,772	15.5.3161	18.2.3066	13.1.3064	−221
1,118,952	18.11.3161	18.8.3066	13.7.3064	−222
1,118,982	18.12.3161	18.9.3066	13.8.3064	−223
1,119,348	1.1.3163	19.9.3067	13.8.3065	−224
1,122,635	13.4.3172	21.9.3076	13.8.3074	−225
1,123,365	6.5.3174	21.9.3078	13.8.3076	−226
1,123,731	18.5.3175	22.9.3079	13.8.3077	−227
1,126,287	7.8.3182	23.9.3086	13.8.3084	−228
1,126,653	19.8.3183	24.9.3087	13.8.3085	−229
1,129,575	21.11.3191	26.9.3095	13.8.3093	−230
1,130,670	24.12.3194	26.9.3098	13.8.3096	−231
1,131,766	29.1.3198	27.9.3101	13.8.3099	−232
1,131,908	23.6.3198	14.2.3102	5.13.3099	−234

APPENDIX II

Ahaziah, king of Israel, dies. Jehoram, the son of Ahab, sole king of Israel
in Samaria two ⭐ years from line 202 (I Ki. 22.52, II Ki. 1.17) . . . . . . –203
Jehoshaphat's death; Jehoram, the son of Jehoshaphat, head of the royal
house of Judah 3 ⭐ years from line 203 (I Ki. 22.42, II Chr. 20.31) . . . . –204
Jehoram, the son of Jehoshaphat, dies; Ahaziah, the son of Jehoram, head
of the royal house of Judah; Joash, the son of Ahaziah, is born. 8 ⭐ years
from line 204 (II Ki. 8.25-26, 9.29, II Chr. 21.5).. . . . . –205
Jehoram, the son of Ahab, dies; Jehu king of Israel; Ahaziah of Judah dies;
Athaliah, his mother, becomes regent in Judah. One ⭐ year from line 205
(II Chr. 22.2) . . . . –206
Athaliah's death; Joash, her grandson, king of Judah six ⭐ years from
line 206 (II Ki. 11.21, 12.1) . . . . –207
Amaziah born 15 ⭐ years from line 207 . . . . –208
Jehoahaz, the son of Jehu, made king of Israel 19 ⭐ years from line 207 . . –209
Jehu's death; Jehoahaz sole king of Israel 3 ⭐ years from line 209 (II Ki.
10.36, 13.1). . . . . –210
Jehoash (Joash), the son of Jehoahaz, made king of Israel 9 ⭐ years from
line 210 . . . . –211
Amaziah made king of Judah two ⭐ years from line 211 . . . . –212
Jehoahaz, the son of Jehu, dies; Jehoash (Joash) and Jeroboam II, sons of
Jehoahaz, co-regents of Israel 3 ⭐ years from line 212 (II Ki. 13.10) . . . –213
Joash, the son of Ahaziah of Judah, dies; Amaziah head of the royal house
of Judah 4 ⭐ years from line 213 (II Ki. 14.2, II Chr. 24.1) . . . . –214
Uzziah (Azariah) born 6 ⭐ years from line 214 . . . . –215
Joash (Jehoash), the son of Jehoahaz, dies; Jeroboam II sole king of Israel
7 ⭐ years from line 214 (II Ki. 14.23). . . . . –216
Uzziah (Azariah) made king of Judah as a child 3 ⭐ years and 7 months
from line 215 . . . . –217
Amaziah's death; Uzziah (Azariah) head of the royal house of Judah 16 ⭐
years from line 215 (II Ki. 14.17, 14.21, 15.1, II Chr. 25.1, 25.25, 26.1) . . . –218
Jotham, the son of Uzziah (Azariah), born 27 ⭐ years from line 217 . . . –219
Zachariah made king of Israel 25 ⭐ years from line 218 (II Ki. 15.8) . . –220
Jeroboam II dies; Zachariah sole king of Israel one year from line 220 . . . –221
Zachariah's death. Shallum king of Israel 6 months (180 days) from line 221
(II Ki. 15.13) . . . . –222
Shallum's death. Menahem king of Israel one month (30 days) from line 222 –223
Ahaz born one ⭐ year from line 223. . . . . –224
Menahem's death. Pekahiah king of Israel 10 ⭐ years from line 223
(II Ki. 15.17). . . . . –225
Pekahiah's death. Pekah king of Israel two ⭐ years from line 225 (II Ki.
15.23, 15.27) . . . . –226
Uzziah's (Azariah's) death; Jotham, the son of Uzziah, king of Judah 52 ⭐
years from line 217. Line 227 is one ⭐ year from line 226 . . . . –227
Hezekiah born 7 ⭐ years from line 227 (II Ki. 15.32). . . . . –228
Ahaz, the son of Jotham, made king of Judah 8 ⭐ years from line 227 . . –229
Jotham's death. Ahaz head of the royal house of Judah 8 ⭐ years from line
229 (II Ki. 16.1, II Chr. 27.1) . . . . –230
Pekah's death. Hoshea king of Israel 3 ⭐ years from line 230 (II Ki. 15.30,
II Ki. 17.1) . . . . –231
Hezekiah made king of Judah 3 ⭐ years from line 231 (II Ki. 18.1, 18.9) . . –232
The beginning of Hezekiah's day of passover. The common meal was at the
end of that day, i.e. at the beginning of the 3100th ⭐ year from line 1 (II
Chr. 29, II Chr. 30) . . . . –234

	☽	☉	✶	
1,132,862	4.3.3201	28.9.3104	13.8.3102	−235
1,133,958	8.4.3204	29.9.3107	13.8.3105	−236
1,135,419	24.5.3208	30.9.3111	13.8.3109	−237
1,140,532	4.11.3222	3.10.3125	13.8.3123	238
1,141,628	8.12.3225	4.10.3128	13.8.3126	−239
1,146,011	25.4.3238	7.10.3140	13.8.3138	−240
1,158,064	13.5.3272	15.10.3173	13.8.3171	−241
1,163,908	16.11.3288	19.10.3189	13.8.3187	−242
1,166,100	25.1.3295	21.10.3195	13.8.3193	−243
1,166,830	17.2.3297	21.10.3197	13.8.3195	−244
1,169,112	28.7.3303	18.1.3204	13.11.3201	−245
1,169,752	19.5.3305	23.10.3205	13.8.3203	−246
1,171,297	30.9.3309	13.1.3210	7.11.3207	−247
1,173,196	11.2.3315	27.3.3215	14.1.3213	−248
1,174,681	21.4.3319	22.4.3219	8.2.3217	−249
1,175,686	23.2.3322	22.1.3222	13.11.3219	−250
1,178,153	12.2.3329	29.10.3228	13.8.3226	−251
1,178,243	14.5.3329	24.1.3229	13.11.3226	−252
1,178,608	25.5.3330	24.1.3230	13.11.3227	−253
1,179,439	30.9.3332	5.5.3232	18.2.3230	−254
1,179,704	29.6.3333	25.1.3233	13.11.3230	−255
1,179,804	11.10.3333	5.5.3233	18.2.3231	−256
1,180,800	4.8.3336	26.1.3236	13.11.3233	−257
1,182,261	20.9.3340	27.1.3240	13.11.3237	−258
1,182,351	21.12.3340	27.4.3240	8.2.3238	−259
1,182,361	2.1.3341	7.5.3240	18.2.3238	−260
1,183,789–90	14.1.3345	5.4.3244	15.1.3242	−262
1,183,803–4	28.1.3345	19.4.3244	29.1.3242	−263
1,184,193–4	5.3.3346	14.5.3245	24.2.3243	−265
1,184,233–4	15.4.3346	24.6.3245	4.4.3243	−266
1,184,294–5	17.6.3346	25.8.3245	5.6.3243	−267
1,184,611–2	10.5.3347	7.7.3246	17.4.3244	269
1,185,515–6	29.11.3349	1.13.3248	10.10.3246	−272
1,185,882–3	12.12.3350	3.13.3249	12.10.3247	−274
1,185,945–6	16.2.3351	1.3.3250	15.12.3247	−276
1,185,959–60	1.3.3351	15.3.3250	29.12.3247	−277
1,185,973	15.3.3351	29.3.3250	7–8.1.3248	−278
1,186,297	14.2.3352	18.2.3251	1–2.12.3248	−280

APPENDIX II

Shalmaneser comes up against Hoshea and begins the siege of Samaria 3 ☆ years from line 232........................ −235
Fall of Samaria 3 ☆ years from line 235 .... −236
Ahaz' death; Hezekiah head of the royal house of Judah 4 ☆ years from line 236................................. −237
Isaiah, the son of Amoz, comes to Hezekiah. (II Ki. 20.1, 20.6) ..... −238
Manasseh born 3 ☆ years from line 238 .... −239
Hezekiah's death; Manasseh king of Judah 15 ☆ years from line 238 (II Ki. 18.2, II Chr. 29.1)........................... −240
Amon born 33 ☆ years from line 240.................. −241
Josiah born 16 ☆ years from line 241 .... −242
Manasseh's death; Amon king of Judah 55 ☆ years from line 240 (II Ki. 21.1, II Chr. 33.1).............................. −243
Amon's death; Josiah king of Judah two ☆ years from line 243 (II Ki. 21.19, II Chr. 33.21)................................ −244
Jehoiakim born............................... −245
Jehoahaz born............................... −246
Beginning of the work of Jeremiah (Jer. 25.3)............. −247
The beginning of Josiah's day of passover (II Chr. 35.1, II Chr. 35.18–19). −248
Zedekiah born............................... −249
Jehoiachin born 18 ☆ years from line 245.............. −250
Josiah's death; Jehoahaz (Shallum) king of Judah 31 ☆ years from line 244 (II Ki. 22.1, II Chr. 34.1)........................ −251
Jehoahaz (Shallum) is dethroned; Jehoiakim king of Judah three months (90 days) from line 251 (II Ki. 23.31, II Chr. 36.2) .... −252
Jehoiachin (Jeconiah or Coniah) made king of Judah one ☆ year from line 252................................... −253
Nebuchadnezzar made king in Babel; Jeremiah prophesies about the royal house of Babel, about the Babylonians, and the children of Israel 23 ☽ years from line 247................................. −254
The beginning of the seventy years of exile. Jehoiakim is carried away (for a short time) to Babel. 3 ☆ years from line 253 (Jer. 25.3, 25.11) ..... −255
Nebuchadnezzar sole king of Babel one ☆ year from line 254 ...... −256
Jehoiakim rebels against Nebuchadnezzar 3 ☆ years from line 255 .... −257
Jehoiakim's death; Jehoiachin (Jeconiah or Coniah) head of the royal house of Judah 4 ☆ years from line 257 (II Ki. 23.36, II Chr. 36.5) .... −258
Jehoiachin's (Jeconiah's or Coniah's) imprisonment; Zedekiah pretender to the throne three months from line 258 (II Ki. 24.8) .... −259
Jehoiachin is dethroned and carried away; Zedekiah sole king of Judah 7 ☆ years from line 256. (II Chr. 36.9–10) .... −260
Ezekiel's first vision in the 30th ☆ year from line 248 (Ez. 1.1) ..... −262
Ezekiel on his left side—in the morning .... −263
Ezekiel on his right side—in the morning—390 days from line 263. (From the middle of this period of 390 days a measure is taken to line 167.) ... −265
Ezekiel gets up—in the morning—40 days from line 265 .... −266
Ezekiel sees the abominations (Ez. 8)................. −267
Ezekiel's prophecy about Israel and Judah (Ez. 20.1).......... −269
The Babylonians come up against Jerusalem (Ez. 24.1)........ −272
Ezekiel's prophecy about Egypt (Ez. 29.1) .... −274
Ezekiel's prophecy about Egypt (Ez. 31.1) .... −276
Ezekiel's prophecy about Tyre (Ez. 26.1)............... −277
Ezekiel's prophecy about Egypt (Ez. 30.20).............. −278
Ezekiel's lamentation for Pharaoh (Ez. 32.1) .... −280

APPENDIX II

	☽	☉	✶	
1,186,310–1	27.2.3352	1.3.3251	15.12.3248	−281
1,186,351–2	9.4.3352	12.4.3251	20.1.3249	−282
1,186,379	7–8.5.3352	10.5.3251	18.2.3249	−283
1,186,524–5	5.10.3352	5.10.3251	13.7.3249	−284
1,191,210	1.1.3366	6.8.3264	10–11.5.3262	−287
1,191,918–9	1.1.3368	14.7.3266	19.4.3264	−290
1,195,454	25–26.12.3377	20.3.3276	27.12.3273	−294
1,204,219	30.9.3402	25.3.3300	26.12.3297	−296
1,204,484	29.6.3403	20.12.3300	16.9.3298	−297
1,204,485–6	1.7.3403	21.12.3300	17.9.3298	−298
1,204,494	9–10.7.3403	30.12.3300	26.9.3298	−299
1,204,499	15.7.3403	5.13.3300	1.10.3298	−300

APPENDIX II

Ezekiel's lamentation for Pharaoh and Egypt (Ez. 32.17) . . . . −281
Fall of Jerusalem; Zedekiah escapes from Jerusalem (Jer. 52.6). . . . . . −282
Nebuzar-adan arrives at Jerusalem; the captured king Zedekiah is deposed
and carried away 11 ⚹ years from line 260 (II Ki. 24.17–18, II Chr. 36.11) −283
Ezekiel is informed about the fall of Jerusalem (Ez. 33.21) . . . . −284
Ezekiel's vision of the new Temple (Ez. 40.1) . . . . −287
Ezekiel's prophecy about Egypt (Ez. 29.17) . . . . −290
(II Ki. 25.27, Jer. 52.31). Jehoiachin's confinement is mitigated . . . . . −294
The beginning of the first year of Cyrus' reign in Babel 70 ☽ years from line
254 (II Chr. 36.21–22) . . . . −296
The end of the seventy years of exile that started in the 3333rd ☽ years. The
first contingent of the people returns 70 ☽ years from line 255 . . . . . . −297
Burnt offerings at the beginning of the 7th month (Ezra 3.6) . . . . . . −298
Day of Atonement begins . . . . −299
The beginning of the Feast of Tabernacles in the ☽ calendar. At sunset at the
beginning of the last day of the thirty-third ☉ century from Era Mundus
(from 'the beginning') . . . . −300